Ēl Shaddai

Honoring His Holy Name

S. Richard Nelson

Other Books by S. Richard Nelson

The Powerful Christian Series:

    Turning Faith into Power

    Gaining Power through Prayer

    The Added Power of Obedience

    The Healing Power of Forgiveness

    The Mighty Power of the Word

    The Gift and Power of the Holy Spirit

    Love: The Only True Power

Sustainable Spirituality

The Faith Factor

Copyright © 2021 by Green Stem Media

All rights reserved. Except as permitted under the United States Copyright Act of 1976, and in the case of brief quotations embodied in critical articles and reviews, no part of this publication may be copied, reproduced or distributed in any form or by any means, or stored in a database or retrieval system, without the prior written authorization from the author.

First Edition published September 2021.

ISBN-13: 978-1-7342387-4-7
ISBN-10: 1734238747
BISAC: Religion / Christian Life / Spiritual Growth

*"From this broken hill,
All your praises they shall ring."*

L. Cohen – If It Be Your Will

Green Stem Media
A Broken Hill Publication

www.greenstemmedia.com
www.srnelson.com

"O Lord our Lord, how excellent is thy name in all the earth!"

Psalms 81:1

"In these names there is a progressive revelation of Jehovah meeting every need as it arises in the experience of His redeemed people—saving, sustaining, strengthening, sanctifying and so on; and not only for the redeemed of that day but for God's saints of all ages."

Nathan Stone, *Names of God*.

God shows us how much He loves us and how much He is doing for us through the exploration of what His many names reveal about Him.

This work is lovingly dedicated to my wife, and my grateful appreciation goes to her and to God for the writing of it.

After hearing the song, *El Shaddai*, my wife suggested I write a "small booklet" about God's names. That idea became the impetus for this book that you are now holding—and quite possibly other volumes to follow.

Writing this book has been the most insightful work I have ever done in developing a deeper, more meaningful relationship with my God and Savior. It is my sincere prayer that it will do the same for you.

Table of Contents

Who Is God to You? 13

My Name is The Lord 19

I Am Jehovah 27

Ēl - The Father of Creation 35

Ēlohim – The Supreme God 41

"Jehovah Jireh, My Son" 49

Shades of Ēl-Shaddai 61

My Foundation, Adonai 71

Look to Jehovah Nissi 81

Ēl-'Elyon, the Most High 91

Alpha and Omega 107

Jehovah Maccaddeshem 115

Ēl-Roi Sees Us 123

Yahweh Rohi – My Shepherd 133

Erkamka – I Love You 142

Yahweh Rapha – Our Healer 146

Abba: More than 'Daddy' 162

Yahweh Shalom is Peace 178

Son of Man-The Messiah 192

Yeshua Saves! 208

The God Ēl 216

Jehovah – Our God 228

Praise His Name 240

Taking On His Name 246

His Name… in Vain 250

Biblical Names of God 256

A Final Word 272

Sample Chapter 278

Preface

Who Is God to You?

Throughout history, God has sought to build strong relationships with His people. Long before He sent His Son to earth, God began revealing Himself to mankind. One of the most significant methods He used was through sharing His personal name. Each divine name reveals to us some quality or characteristic of God. Divine names identify and elevate Him infinitely higher than all other beings, whether in Heaven or on earth.

God's names accentuate traits and offer promises for our good. Studying God's divine names is a valuable way to discover and experience unique aspects of His character. As we identify and embrace these characteristics, we will be drawn into a closer relationship with our Heavenly Father.

Each name that God uses for Himself reveals an aspect of His character that helps us to know Him better. The noun "God" is a title. The Bible employs various names for God that convey specific, personal meaning and identity. The meanings behind God's names reveal to us His fundamental personality and nature.

There is extreme power in a name. The dictionary describes "name" as authority and character. A name denotes who we are. It is what we are known by to all around us. In Old Testament times, a name was more than a mere identification; it was an identity as well. Names had special meanings attached to them and often carried an explanatory purpose.

A name can indicate physical characteristics as seen in the case of Esau.

"And the first came out reddish all over, like a hairy garment; so they named him Esau." [1]

Esau means "hairy", which was one of his physical characteristics when he was born. Later, he was also called Edom, meaning "red." [2]

---

[1] Gen. 25:25.
[2] Gen. 25:30.

The name Jacob means "supplanter, deceiver, defrauder." Esau said of him: "Jacob is the right name for him! He has supplanted me two times! He took away my birthright, and now, look, he has taken away my blessing." [3] Later, when Jacob wrestled with God and prevailed, God changed Jacob's name to Israel:

"Your name will no longer be called Jacob but Israel, for you have fought with God and with men, and have prevailed." [4] Israel has been variously translated to mean "Prince with God," "Soldier of God," or "One who wrestles with God." Jacob's name was changed to suit his new character.

Changing a name often accompanied a change of position or character. Jesus changed Simon's name to Peter [5] meaning "stone" or "rock." Simon's new name described something solid, steady, and firm, which he became.

The fact that a name reveals character is true for people as well as for God. Throughout scripture God reveals Himself to us through His nearly 1000 names. God's names are descriptions of His character and nature, and there is nothing so powerful as the name of God. The Bible declares that "the name of the Lord

---

[3] Gen. 27:36.
[4] Gen. 32:28.
[5] Matt. 10:2.

is like a strong tower; the righteous person runs to it and is set safely on high." [6]

When Jesus declared: "I have come in my Father's name," [7] He was stating that He came with His Father's authority, but an added meaning to that statement is that He came to manifest His Father's character. Jesus portrayed the Father to such a degree that He could say: "The Father and I are one." [8] and "the person who has seen me has seen the Father." [9] The words that Jesus spoke were the words His Father gave Him to speak [10] and the works that He did were those given to Him by the Father. [11]

No one name could ever reveal the full nature of God, but in the Bible, God reveals himself through many names. Each one of His names is used to reveal another distinct part of his character and nature.

So, who is God to you?

Is He *Ēlohim*, your Most High God,

---

[6] Pro. 18:10.
[7] John 5:43.
[8] John 10:30.
[9] John 14:9.
[10] See John 3:34; 8:28; 8:38; 12:50; 14:10; 17:8.
[11] See John 5:36; 9:4; 17:4.

Jehovah Shalom, the Lord of Peace,

Ēl Shaddai, the All Sufficient One,

Jehovah Jireh, the Lord Who Will Provide,

Adonai, the Lord Over All,

Jehovah Raah, the Lord our Shepherd?

Jesus addressed Him perfectly when He called Him, *Abba*, our Father. Our Father is the ultimate source of all attributes and powers of life, and He is the Supreme Intelligence over everything. We hold the promise that our Father's love is everlasting, His mercies are renewed every morning, and His faithfulness is great.

God's name is of paramount importance. Nehemiah declares: "May your glorious name be blessed; may it be lifted up above all blessing and praise." [12]

To hallow a thing is to make it holy, to set it apart to be exalted and worthy of absolute devotion. To hallow the name of God is to regard Him with complete devotion and loving admiration. We should preserve His name in a position of solemn significance in our

---

[12] Neh. 9:5.

hearts and minds. We should rejoice in it and think deeply about its true meaning.

Jesus told us to "love the Lord your God with all your heart, with all your soul, with all your mind, and with all your strength." [13] An excellent way to practice that daily is to know God's very character through the power of His name. When we search and study the names that He reveals to us in the Bible, we will better understand who God really is.

God's names, character and nature remain the same through all generations. He is completely trustworthy, all powerful, eternally loving, and constantly present. If we need reassurance and greater faith today, we can find hope in His powerful name. He is the God of miracles. Nothing is impossible for Him.

---

[13] Mark 12:30.

Chapter One

My Name is The Lord

I have a friend who named his son after his eleventh-generation grandfather, the first of his adventurous ancestors to leave the shackles of the old world and pursue the religious freedoms of a new and undiscovered land. But then, in contrast, he named his daughter after a Cat Stevens' song. In today's culture and society, names are often selected based on popularity, current societal trends, in honor of an ancestor or simply on how pleasant the name sounds.

It seems that these days names are just a *flatus vocis*, a mere sound. The tendency to reduce language to some whimsical standard with no regard for its profound origins appears suggestive of human secularization and the seeming triviality of life itself. It reflects a weakening in the religious consciousness where, anciently, names were thought to be of divine origin.

Many parents today, my friend included obviously, do not hold the same regard or significance to naming a child as did their predecessors. Anciently, names were used not only to identify but also to describe, depict and define. The giving of a name was considered a sacred and significant occasion. In ancient times, a name was a portrayal of a person's nature. To declare that name was to reveal and make known the true self.

The Hebrew word for name is *shem*, meaning "memorial." In Biblical writing, a name memorialized something about the personality, character, experience, or occupation of a person. A name would capture the essence or nature of an individual. Parents often chose a name they hoped the child would live up to. Regularly, parents named a child based on the circumstances surrounding its birth.

Rachel named her son *Ben-Oni,* meaning the "son of my sorrow," because the delivery was so difficult that, in the end, it took her life. [14]

---

[14] Gen. 35:18.

Hannah named her boy *Samuel* which means, "heard of God," since she felt that the child was an answer to her prayers. [15]

Jabez was so named because his mother "experienced pain" when she gave birth to him. [16]

Hagar named her child *Ishmael* or "the Lord hears," as a token of the fact that God had heard her and would continue to hear her in her afflictions. [17]

After her husband had been killed, her nation defeated, the ark of the covenant captured, and the death of her father-in-law, Phinehas's pregnant wife delivered a son whom she named, just before she died, *Ichabod*, meaning "the glory has departed." [18]

Rachel named her firstborn son *Joseph*, meaning "he shall increase," believing that God would give her yet another son. [19]

In Old Testament times, a person's name often reflected his or her character.

Abraham means "Father of a great multitude."

---

[15] 1 Sam. 1:20.
[16] 1 Chron. 4:9.
[17] Gen. 16:11.
[18] 1 Sam. 4:21.
[19] Gen. 30:24.

Eve means "Living," which is fitting because she is the mother of all living people.

Jesus means "Savior."

Names could point to a person's disposition, career, calling in life, and more. Nowhere in all history is the significance of properly descriptive, illustrative names more evident than in the names of Deity. Moses understood this.

When the Lord called Moses from the burning bush and commissioned him to bring the Hebrew people out of Egypt, Moses asked God:

"If I go to the Israelites and tell them, 'The God of your fathers has sent me to you,' and they ask me, 'What is his name?'—what should I say to them?"

Recognizing the extreme importance the Hebrews ascribed to names, Moses fully anticipated that his people would ask in whose name he acted. He is asking God to provide some credibility to the fantastic story he's about to tell his people. Essentially, he's asking God about his true character and nature.

Responding, the Lord said:

"I AM THAT I AM."

Moses was then instructed to say:

"The Lord—the God of your fathers, the God of Abraham, the God of Isaac, and the God of Jacob—has sent me to you. This is my name forever, and this is my memorial from generation to generation." [20]

The numerous names of God show us the various perceptions of Deity. Within the two passages just quoted, the personality of God is distinctly expressed. *I AM* is the first-person singular form of the verb "to be." It implies His eternal nature.

In the name I AM, or Jehovah (Jehovah is the English rendering of the Hebrew tetragram YHWH or JHWH), God manifests Himself as a personal living being who labors for Israel and who will fulfill the promises made to their fathers. All of this conveys the idea of an unchanging, ever-living God, who through all generations is true to His word.

God's name is I AM, not I was, not I might be, not maybe I'll get around to it. God is, always was and always will be.

"God's personal existence, the continuity of His dealings with man, the unchangeableness of His promises, and the whole revelation of His redeeming mercy, gather around the name Jehovah." [21]

To declare the name of the Lord is to testify of the Lord.

---

[20] Exo. 3:13-15.
[21] Source Unknown.

"For this purpose," the Lord told Moses, "have I caused you to stand: to show you my strength, and so that my name may be declared in all the earth." [22]

Jeremiah foretold of a time when the nations would come from the ends of the earth. The Lord told Jeremiah: "I will this once cause them to know, I will cause them to know mine hand and my might; and they shall know that my name is The Lord." [23]

The myriad names of God can help us to experience God's majesty and the deep and abiding love He feels for us. God reveals His wonderful names to us so that we may encounter and experience Him in all these ways. While it is marvelous to read the inspiring names of God in the Bible, our true purpose is to come to know God on a personal level.

He wants to reveal Himself to us in ways that will amaze and astonish us. As we read through and study the various names of God from Hebrew and Holy Scripture, we can better allow His presence to saturate our lives. We can enhance our relationship with God as we come to accurately understand the many aspects of His holy names. He longs for us to know Him to the

---

[22] Exo. 9:16.
[23] Jer. 16:21. (KJV)

fullest. These names reveal who God wants to be for you and for me.

Chapter Two

I Am Jehovah

God has no shortage of names—He is called by almost 1000 different names in the Bible.

But one of these names stands above all others. Jehovah, or *Yahweh*, is perhaps the most important of the Old Testament names for God. *I AM* is regarded by many to be the ultimate name of God. *Yahweh* was considered so sacred by the Hebrews that it was customary not to pronounce it out loud when speaking or reading but to replace it with the word *Adonai*, meaning Lord.

The English language doesn't have an exact translation of the word *Yahweh*. Consequently, in our Old Testament we see it written as *LORD* in all capital letters.

The vowels for the name *YHWH* had to be supplied by the person reading the sacred texts. The name Jehovah, it is believed, originated around 1500 A.D. by combining the consonants *JHVH* with the vowels from the word *Adonai*.

YHWH is the proper name for the Hebrew God. It appears 6,828 times in the Old Testament (almost 700 times in the Psalms alone). Yahweh is the Self-existent One. He exists eternally. Consequently, He will always exist. We can always have faith in and rely on Him because He is our eternal source of strength. [24]

Theologically, the name *Yahweh* resonates with covenant: "I will take you to myself as a people, and I will be your God." [25]

Yahweh is the name of the God of the Covenant. He only uses this name with the people who know Him and who are in covenant with Him. Yahweh is the covenant-keeping name.

God calls Himself *Yahweh* when He enters into the covenant with Abraham, a subtle promise that He will forever be faithful in keeping His word. When He reveals Himself again as *Yahweh* to Moses, it is a reminder that He is unchanging, and we can trust Him not to back out of or break His promises to us.

---

[24] Gen. 2:4; Isa. 40:3,10; 1 Sam. 1:20; Exo. 6:1-4, 3:1-22.
[25] Exo. 6:7.

God revealed Himself to Moses from the burning bush as "I AM that I AM," in other words, the Self-existing One. [26] I am God because I exist eternally. In so doing, God made it clear to Moses that He is eternally present. God has always existed. He existed then, He exists now, and He will continue to exist forever.

This name Jehovah holds within it this quality of self-existence. Immediately following the verse that reveals the name, God also declares: "this is my name forever." [27] All subsequent names of God, therefore, should include the idea of the ever-present, self-existing God.

Heraclitus stated: "There is nothing permanent except change." Our world is constantly shifting; in flux; subjective. Things change from day to day. But God does not. He remains constant through it all. He doesn't change His nature based on new and popular philosophies and theologies. From the very beginning of time, *Yahweh* has always been who He is; He has always been the standard of perfection and holiness.

YAH is an abbreviated rendering that appears fifty times in the Old Testament, often in the admonition *hallelu-jah* (literally, "Praise *Yah*").

---

[26] Exo. 3:14.
[27] Exo. 3:15.

The etymology as well as the context in which the name is disclosed suggests "presence." *Yahweh* or Jehovah defines God's eternal presence with His people. He is always here to aid and assist us, to comfort and console us, to guide and direct us, to elevate and enlightened us. God is "with us," as in the promised name Immanuel—*God with us.* [28] He is near His people. *Yahweh* is present, accessible, and close to those who call on Him [29] for deliverance, [30] forgiveness, [31] and guidance. [32] His presence and His influence never departs. He never leaves us. The greatest comfort we can ever find in this life is found in the very name of God: *I AM*.

The name *YHWH* defines Him as deeply involved in our human struggles. The promise of salvation presented in Exodus 6:6-8 is expansive, including intimacy with God and blessings of abundance, but it is decidedly bracketed first and last with "I am *Yahweh*."

"Therefore, tell the Israelites, '*I am Yahweh*, and I will bring you out from under the burdens of the Egyptians, and I will rid you out of their bondage, and I

---

[28] Isa. 7:14; Matt. 1:23.
[29] Psalms 145:18.
[30] Psalms 107:13.
[31] Psalms 25:11.
[32] Psalms 31:3.

will redeem you with an outstretched arm, and with great judgments:

"And I will take you to me for a people, and I will be to you a God; and you shall know that I am *Yahweh* your God, who brings you out from under the burdens of the Egyptians.

"I will bring you into the land which I swore to give to Abraham, to Isaac, and to Jacob; and I will give it to you for a heritage: *I am Yahweh.*'" [33]

In the Bible, *Yahweh* is used when the author is writing about God's personal relationship with His people. A prime example of this is the 19th Psalm. The first 6 verses speak of *Ēlohim* and His connection with the physical world. Verse 7 however, suddenly shifts to *Yahweh* and His relationship with those who know Him and who are in covenant with Him. *Yahweh* is an intensely personal God, seeking to have a relationship with His people.

God will never stop wanting us, and He will never cease in His pursuit of us. He is so motivated by His love for us that He agreed to pay the consequence of the punishment we deserve.

This is our relational God. This is *Yahweh*.

---

[33] Exo. 6:6-8. WEB, Italics added.

Jesus of Nazareth stunned and astounded the religious leaders of Israel with an unprecedented declaration never articulated since the beginning of time. Jesus Christ asserted that He is God, when He proclaimed:

"...before Abraham was, I AM." [34]

In so asserting, Jesus claimed the very name of the Hebrew Old Testament God! Jesus Christ is *YHWH*, or I AM. By applying the name *Yahweh* to Himself, Jesus affirmed that He is God. To the Judeans this was the highest form of blasphemy. When the Pharisees heard it, they picked up stones to kill Jesus.

The resurrected Lord later revealed Himself to the apostle John in the book of Revelation with a name comparable to the name "I AM." To John He said:

"I am the Alpha and the Omega... the one who is, and who was, and who is still to come, the All-Powerful!" [35]

Jesus Christ left no doubt that He is I AM, the same who appeared to Moses. He is the one who always existed, and He is the one who will always be.

---

[34] John 8:58.
[35] Rev. 1:8.

"The name carries overtones of presence, salvation defined as deliverance and blessing, covenantal bondedness, and integrity." [36]

Yahweh is a paradox; a God of mystery, yet a God who is closer than our very breath. Our daily goal, our daily desire should be to move one step closer to knowing the God who exists. The richness and fullness of perfect love await those seeking to know Him.

His love is worth the pursuit.

Remember that God is real. The names that follow reveal who *He* wants to be for us, in our lives and in the lives of our loved ones.

---

[36] Bakers Evangelical Dictionary.

Chapter Three

Ēl - The Father of Creation

The miniscule word אל (*Ēl*) is very common in the Hebrew language and has a great many meanings. In the Western Semitic world, the word *Ēl* was used to refer to a god or a deity. *Ēl* was both a generic word for any god and the special name or title of a particular god who was distinguished from other gods as being "the God." The etymology of the word is uncertain, but its root seems to designate power or might.

The word *Ēl* was used not only in the Hebrew Bible but also in Akkadian, Phoenician, and various Semitic languages. *Ēl* was venerated as a high god by many in the Ancient Near East throughout the second millennium B.C. The word *Ēl* is listed at the head of many temples or pantheons.

Most knowledge surrounding the god *Ēl* comes from Canaanite literature found at Ugarit dating to the Late Bronze Age. In some Canaanite and Ugaritic sources, *Ēl* played a role as the father of the gods or father of creation. *Ēl* could refer to any god, but it was also the designated name of a particular god in the Canaanite pantheon. *Ēl* was the supreme god of the Canaanites.

In the English language, the word or title "God" exclusively refers to deity but in Hebrew the word is far more common and may express approach and negation, acts of wailing and pointing, and may even signify an oak or terebinth tree. It is also found in ancient Hebrew compound names like "*Isra-Ēl*" (prince of *Ēl*) and "*Beth-Ēl*" (house of *Ēl*).

The word *Ēl* is found throughout the Old Testament (except the book of Leviticus) and is considered the most primitive Hebrew name for God. In the Hebrew Bible, the word *Ēl* is generally used as a designation of a deity, whether it be of the true God, or of false gods, or even of the idols used in pagan worship. However, the name *Ēl* usually refers to and is the generally accepted shortened form of אלהים (*Ēlohim*), the genus God.

Abraham, Isaac and Jacob worshiped only one God, not many. Since Abraham did not know God's real name, he may have acknowledged *Ēl* as the God who appeared to him. [37] However, the Biblical text emphasizes that the God Abraham worshiped was not the same God that the Canaanites worshiped. While Abraham's forefathers most likely worshiped the moon god venerated in Haran, [38] the God of the patriarchs was the God who appeared to Abraham.

The early Israelites, not knowing the real name of God, believed that God was *Ēl* who had brought them out of Egypt. *Yahweh* told Moses that in the days of the patriarchs, He revealed His name to them as *Ēl*:

"God spoke to Moses and said to him, 'I am *Yahweh*. To Abraham, Isaac and Jacob I appeared as *Ēl Shaddai*, but I did not make my name *Yahweh* known to them.'" [39]

Ēl is known as the supreme God. He is the father of all humanity and the creator deity. He is known for His tremendous power and strength. After revealing His name to Moses, the name *Ēl* and its compounds became associated with *Yahweh*, the God of Israel, and were less used in reference to the God of their ancestors.

Biblical writers often used *Ēl* to designate the one true God, a God separate from and superior to the

---

[37] See Exo. 6:2, 3.
[38] Josh.24:2.
[39] Exo. 6:2, 3 (NJB).

gods of the ancient Near East. In the eyes of the Israelites, Jehovah or *Yahweh* was the God of gods, the great, mighty, and powerful *Ēl*. [40] He was also proclaimed as "The *Ēl* of the *elim*" or "The God of the gods." [41]

In the patriarchal writings, when reference to the Israelite God *Ēlohim* needed to be abbreviated (to serve as part of a compound name), the result was the name *Ēl*. *Ēl* was used together with other epithets of God to designate and identify the God worshiped by Abraham, Isaac and Jacob. We often discover the personal character of *Ēlohim* when we see the word shortened to *Ēl* and then coupled with another word, as in *Ēl -Shaddai, Ēl -Roi,* or *Ēl -Elyon*.

God's many names reflect the Semitic culture of Abraham, Isaac and Jacob and emphasize the essential function and responsibility that *Ēl* retained in the religion of the Hebrews. Other names of God compounded with the word *Ēl* include:

Ēl Elyon, meaning "God Most High." [42] This name is connected to Abraham, Melchizedek and the city of Salem (Jerusalem).

---

[40] Deut. 10:17.
[41] Dan. 11:36.
[42] Gen.14:18-22.

Ēl Roi, is translated as "The God Who Sees." [43] This name relates to a well located between Kadesh and Bered.

Ēl Olam, translated as "The Everlasting God." [44]

Ēl Elohe Israel, which means "God, the God of Israel." [45]

Ēl Berith denotes the god worshiped by the indigenous Canaanite population at Shechem. [46]

Several Old Testament characters have *Ēl* in their name: Elijah meaning "*Ēl* is *Yahweh*" and Samuel, "Heard by *Ēl*" are just two examples of this. Remembering the accounts of both Elijah and Samuel reveals the importance names held in Old Testament times. Elijah is known as the prophet who was steadfast in proclaiming that *Yahweh* was the only true *Ēlohim*.

The Israelites experienced God on a personal level and that experience led them to articulate their deepest feelings about God. If you were to give God a name based on your relationship with Him and your

---

[43] Gen. 16:13.
[44] Gen. 21:33.
[45] Gen. 33:20.
[46] Judges 9:46.

experience with how He interacts in your life, what would His name be for you?

    Ēl My Rock? [47]

    Ēl My Savior? [48]

    The *Ēl* of My Life? [49]

    Ēl Who Fulfills His Purpose for Me? [50]

    Ēl My Strong Refuge? [51]

    Ēl Who Forgives? [52]

    Or the *Ēl* of Our Salvation? [53]

---

[47] Psa. 42:9.
[48] Isa. 12:2; Psa. 106:21.
[49] Psa. 42:8.
[50] Psa. 57:2.
[51] 2 Sam. 22:33.
[52] Psa. 99:8.
[53] Psa. 68:19, 20.

Chapter Four

Ēlohim – The Supreme God

Each of the different names of God highlights an aspect of His eternal character. Biblical writers referenced God with numerous monikers, the most frequent being *Ēlohim* meaning "the strong, creator God." It appears approximately 2,750 times in the Old Testament starting with the very first verse: "In the beginning *Ēlohim* created the heavens and the earth." [54]

The name *Ēlohim* refers to God's incredible power and might. He is the one and only God, the true God in a world that promotes so many false gods. He is the one on whom we can fully rely. He is sovereign, and He is supreme; the one we can completely trust. He is mighty over all of nature, this world, and the heavens

---

[54] Gen. 1:1.

above. He is the creative God who has worked wonders by His hands.

Ēlohim is the creator, powerful and mighty, Lord of lords. He is the Lord Most High, stronger and mightier than anyone or anything. Whenever we face intolerable circumstances or insufferable adversaries, we can be reassured knowing that God is stronger than anything we face. [55] From the Bible's first sentence the superlative nature of God's power is evident as *Ēlohim* speaks a world into existence. [56] His name reflects His power as He enables barren women to conceive, [57] and as He brings the oppressed out of Egypt. [58] The Apostle Peter tells us that believers are protected through faith by God's power. [59] In the name *Ēlohim* is the fullness of divine power. [60]

Interestingly, *Ēlohim* is a plural name, literally meaning "Gods," and this has plagued and puzzled Jewish and Christian scholars extensively in their anxiety to preserve the idea of the oneness of God. Various methods have been sought to explain away the plurality of this word. Primarily, it is interpreted to be

---

[55] Gen. 1:1; 17:7; Psa. 19:1; Jer. 31:33.
[56] Gen. 1:3; 1:6; 1:9.
[57] Gen. 18:10; 18:14; 25:21.
[58] Exo. 20:2.
[59] 1 Pet. 1:5.
[60] Bakers Evangelical Dictionary.

"intensive," and implies a fullness of mind or a richness of attributes.

Ēlohim is always rendered as "God" in the English authorized version, however, the fact remains that Ēlohim is a plural form and properly translated means "Gods." Is this a reference to the Trinity, or Godhead? That interpretation cannot be disproven, but many believe that this is a plural of abstraction: "...that is, 'a more or less intensive focusing of the characteristics inherent in the idea of the stem... Hebrew uses the plural form for abstract nouns such as youth, old age, maidenhood, and life." [61]

The plural name Ēlohim may also possibly represent those who have partaken of the "Divine Nature." Through Christ, God has given to those who receive the gospel "his precious and most magnificent promises, so that by means of what was promised, you may become partakers of the Divine Nature after escaping the worldly corruption that is produced by evil desire." [62]

Evidence that many have attained this Divine Nature is given by reason of a large number of passages from the Old Testament:

---

[61] Frame, John, (Reference Unknown).
[62] See 2 Pet. 1:4.

"For the Lord God is God of gods and Lord of lords." [63]

"The Lord God of gods, he knoweth, and Israel he shall know." [64]

"Give thanks unto the God of gods...give thanks to the Lord of lords." [65]

"He will utter presumptuous things against the God of gods." [66]

Paul's passage in Corinthians harmonizes with these Scriptures:

"If after all there are so-called gods, whether in heaven or on earth (as there are many gods and many lords), yet for us there is one God, the Father, from whom are all things and for whom we live, and one Lord, Jesus Christ, through whom are all things and through whom we live." [67]

Next to *Yahweh*, *Ēlohim* is the major designation for God. *Ēlohim* refers to deity but becomes virtually the name for the one, true God. *Ēlohim* sums up what is intended by the word god or the divine.

---

[63] Deut. 10:17.
[64] Josh. 22:22 (KJV).
[65] Psa.136:2, 3.
[66] Dan. 11:36.
[67] 1 Cor. 8:5.

After the first chapter of Genesis, the name *Ēlohim* seems to be supplanted by "the Lord God," as He was known under that title in Genesis 2 and elsewhere. The name or title appears first in the fourth verse of Genesis 2, an interpretation of the Hebrew "*Ēl-Shaddai*," translated as "God Almighty," and in the New Testament as "God, the Almighty Father."

The significance of the names of God may be understood here in the light of the new knowledge concerning the limitless immensity of God's universe. *Ēlohim* is the word most frequently used when referring to God's dealings with creation in general or with the nations of the world apart from His covenant with Israel. When we experience *Ēlohim* through His power displayed in nature, we will gravitate toward an enlightened concept of *Ēlohim*.

"The heavens declare the glory of God; the sky displays His handiwork." [68]

We can be assured we are upheld by an Almighty God. *Ēlohim's* amazing power is at work in every sunrise and every sunset every day. He holds the stars in the sky, yet He still carries His people through their difficult times. We never have to fear because God's hands are strong and secure.

---

[68] Psa. 19:1.

The discoveries of modern science concerning the immensity of the universe—billions of splendid, blazing suns that inlay the sky of the visible universe which compose our own recognized galaxy, of which there may be endless thousands of such galaxies—and it is conceivable that these billions of blazing suns may be like our own sun, the centers of opaque planets, and they all declare His power.

Ēlohim is the epitome of might and power. Paul teaches us:

"For since the creation of the world his invisible attributes—his eternal power and divine nature—have been clearly seen, because they are understood through what has been made. So that people are without excuse." [69]

From the creation onward, we see God progressively revealing Himself to humanity. As Ēlohim, He places Himself in covenant with His creation; He enters into a special relationship and covenant with Abraham. These covenantal promises [70] find their climax and fulfillment in God's supreme gift; namely, Jesus Christ. It is here that we move from a vague understanding of Ēlohim into a covenantal, relational, and very personal knowledge of God.

---

[69] Rom. 1:20.
[70] See Gen. 12.

God created us. He is *Ēlohim*. He is our father, and we are His children. Yet, simply acknowledging this is not nearly enough. Almost everyone believes in a higher power. Simply knowing that *Ēlohim* exists means that we have merely risen to the same faith as the demons. [71] It is only when we move from the elementary knowledge of *Ēlohim* as Creator that we can begin to embrace the concept of God as our Father.

Too often we suppress that truth in our own unrighteousness. Or we morph *Ēlohim* into a vague notion of a universal power. Our adoration of all-mighty God becomes the worship of some lesser, earthly god who feels more comfortable and easy-going. Or perhaps we suppress any concept of *Ēlohim*, choosing instead to elevate our own might and strength. We make ourselves arbitrators of truth.

A person drowning in a mere ten feet of water isn't in much better shape than a person drowning in a thousand feet of water. Merely acknowledging the existence of God doesn't put us in a better position than those who actively and aggressively deny the concept of God. When our knowledge of *Ēlohim* becomes personal, then we move toward what we would call actual saving faith.

---

[71] James 2:19.

When we fully understand the mighty power of *Ēlohim*, we can declare like the psalmist:

"Help me, oh Lord my God: Oh save me according to thy mercy." [72]

Such a prayer is a reflection of the saving power and knowledge of *Ēlohim*.

How do we really see *Ēlohim*?

Do we know Him simply as the mighty one? Or as a higher universal power?

Or can we declare with all the praise and supplication of an adoring heart: "Oh Lord my God"?

---

[72] Psa. 109:26.

Chapter Five

"Jehovah Jireh, My Son"

What do you think of when you hear the word "provision?" For many of us it is a weightless word.

To a scout it may mean trail mix, a full canteen and a first aid kit. To someone on a road trip it could mean Twizzlers®, GPS and an awesome playlist. To a soldier it could mean MREs, ammo and a powerful weapon.

The provision of the Lord is something quite different—distinct and unique. *Yahweh Yireh* means "The Lord will provide." It means that God will provide for our needs—every one of them. The Hebrew verb *ra'ah* from which *yireh* is derived (translated as "provide" in many modern Bibles) means "to see." God sees the past, present, and future. He is able to see and anticipate everything we need and provide for us.

Some of us have experienced moments when God provided for us in obvious ways; an unexpected check in the mail to cover rent or a friend's generosity paying for a medical expense. We may think of God's provision as unforeseen improvements in our lives as when the Lord provides us with a new car or the means to remodel the house. We recognize these as God's provision, but rarely do we *depend* on provision.

"And my God will supply all your needs according to His glorious riches in Christ Jesus." [73]

Do we ever take this passage for granted? Do we forget the promise God has made to us? Notice the simple yet significant word *all*.

What needs do you have today? What do you want "the Lord who sees" to provide for you today? Whatever it is, make it known to Him. He sees and knows already but making it known to Him is an acknowledgment that you trust Him to provide. God will supply *all* your needs.

Understandably, His timing may be different than ours. We may feel that He's forgotten us or hasn't

---

[73] Phil. 4:19.

even heard our petition. Of course, sometimes we get our "needs" and "wants" mixed up, and other times the Lord who sees knows what is better for us than we even know ourselves. We can trust that all things are possible for Him even when we can't see the solution.

In Matthew, Chapter 6, Jesus teaches that our heavenly Father cares for us and that we need never worry about our provision. He is the very source of our life.

"Do not worry about your life, what you will eat or drink, or about your body, what you will wear...

"Look at the birds in the sky: they do not sow, or reap, or gather into barns, yet your heavenly Father feeds them. Aren't you more valuable than they are...?

...Think about how the flowers of the field grow; they do not work or spin.

"Yet I tell you that not even Solomon in all his glory was clothed like one of these." [74]

In these passages, Jesus teaches us the nature of God's provision. He provides for even the smallest, inconsequential beings in his myriad creations. He clothes them and feeds them. As treasured entities of His creation, His eye is always on them.

---

[74] Matt. 6:25-29.

More than treasured entities, we are His image bearers, uniquely born as His children. So why should we worry about His provision? As any loving father, He provides the best for His children without hesitation and always at the right time.

Nothing will come from worrying but so very much will be provided through Christ if we follow what Jesus asks of us. We needn't waste time worrying, but should, instead, turn our hearts over to God and let *Yahweh Yireh* worry about how He will make the provision.

"But seek first God's kingdom, and his righteousness; and all these things will be added to you.

"So then, do not worry about tomorrow, for tomorrow will worry about itself. Today has enough trouble of its own." [75]

We can walk in peace and confidence knowing that God is in control. This is the personal implication of *Yahweh Yireh.* Everything we need, God will provide. None of us have to go it alone, relying on our meager strength or abilities. We simply need to learn to call on the One who has promised to provide everything we need.

---

[75] Matt. 6:33, 34 (WEB, NET).

Yet too often we only think of God's provision as if He were a waiter at a restaurant. We signal Him to our table, place our orders in faith, and then we receive what we have requested. Occasionally perhaps, we think of God as providing family, friends, employment, daily care, health, church, talents and abilities, and answers to our prayers. All of this is an added share of God's provision to us, but if we stop here, we stop short of the unfathomable experience of what *Yahweh Yireh* actually means in our lives.

Grace in Time of Need

Jesus' sacrifice on our behalf is God's way of providing us access to His grace.

"Let us therefore come boldly to the throne of grace, that we may obtain mercy, and find grace to help in time of need." [76]

Some days we may forget that we have access to the grace of God. *Yahweh Yireh* has provided it for us. The Savior's sacrifice secured it for us. It is not part-time access nor is it provisional access. Whenever we feel the need for God's grace, no matter the time of day, no matter where we find ourselves, full-time access has

---

[76] Heb. 4:16 (WEBSTER).

been provided for us. God has granted it and we should take advantage of what He has provided.

Strength for Our Weakness

Christ's gospel is a gospel of paradoxes: "The first shall be last and the last shall be first." "You must lose your life in order to save it."

Here is another interesting gospel paradox: Our strength does not attract the power of God into our lives, but our weakness does.

"My grace is sufficient for you," the Lord told Paul, "for my power is made perfect in weakness." [77]

God sees and understands our weaknesses. When we look to Him for help, He becomes the Lord who provides strength in our weakness. The simple stipulation is that His strength will come only *after* we acknowledge our weakness. Once we accept that, then *Yahweh Yireh* provides His all-sufficient grace and power to strengthen and assist us to withstand any condition. Acknowledging our weakness allows the Lord who provides to make us strong.

---

[77] 2 Cor. 12:9 (WEB).

A Way Out

God knew that we would face temptations to sin in this life. When we face temptations, we still seem to struggle with our sinful nature.

"No temptation has taken you except what is common to mankind. But God is faithful; he will not let you be tempted beyond what you can bear. But when you are tempted, he will also provide a way out so that you can endure it." [78]

When we are tempted, tested or tried, the Lord who provides will always open a way out, we simply need to look for the exit sign. God has provided an escape so that we needn't become victims to temptation.

The Greatest Provision of All

Genesis, Chapter 22, relates how God commanded Abraham to take his son Isaac to Mount Moriah and offer him as a sacrifice. Isaac was Abraham's son of promise, a miraculous gift from God and God had pledged to make Isaac into a great nation. He was God's provision, or so it seemed, until God asked Abraham to take what he treasured most, his

---

[78] 1 Cor. 10:13.

only son, Isaac, whom he loved so much, into the bleak wilderness of Moriah and offer him up in an act of absolute devotion to the Lord.

"God tested Abraham. He said to him, 'Abraham!' 'Here I am!' Abraham replied.

"God said, 'Take your son—your only son, whom you love, Isaac—and go to the land of Moriah! Offer him up there as a burnt offering on one of the mountains which I will indicate to you.'" [79]

How could God make such a request? Why would He require something so atrocious from a man He called His friend? And yet Abraham, the father of our faith, obeyed God.

Abraham saddled his donkey, hoisting his young son on its back with the sacrificial bundle of wood and set out as the sun was rising over the desert. They certainly made a strange entourage trekking across the barren land with Isaac believing he was on a great adventure with his dad and a couple of their servants.

Three days into the journey, Abraham spotted in the distance the mountain where his promises would die. And still he went on.

When his precious son asked: "My father... where is the lamb for the burnt offering?" Abraham

---

[79] Gen 22:1,2.

must have choked up as he replied: "Jehovah *jireh*" God will provide, my son. [80]

Can you picture the two of them, father and son, walking together toward death? God must have loved His friend in that special moment! Did tears fall from the eyes of the God who weeps as He watched the determined steps of a father willing to let his only son die simply because God asked it of him?

When they arrived at the place which God had appointed, Abraham built an altar, laid the wood in order, bound his son and laid Isaac on top of the wood. Abraham then took out the knife to slaughter his son.

Hebrews, Chapter 11, tells us that Abraham acted on the faith that God would raise Isaac. He obeyed because he believed that the Lord would provide a miracle. And the Lord did provide.

The angel of the Lord called to him from heaven and said, "Abraham!...do not lay your hand on the boy or do anything to him, for now I know that you fear God, seeing you have not withheld your son, your only son, from me." [81]

Abraham lifted up his eyes and found a ram caught in a thicket behind him. Abraham took the ram

---

[80] Gen. 22:7, 8.
[81] Gen. 22:11, 12.

and offered it up as a burnt offering in the place of his son.

Imagine the praise and worshiping that must have taken place on that mountain. Father and son, arms wrapped around each other in heart-pumping relief, weeping, laughing, rejoicing with shouts that echoed off the barren cliff walls. Alone with his son Isaac in the wilderness, Abraham knew and trusted that God would provide a sacrifice. He believed in God's character, and trusted Him to be faithful, loving, and the God who would provide.

"And Abraham called the name of that place 'The Lord provides.' It is said to this day, 'In the mountain of the Lord provision will be made.'" [82]

When Abraham pronounced that powerful statement, "Jehovah *jireh*, my son," it was not in the context of snacks or cars or money for bills. It was in the context of the most profound physical need a person can face—the loss of life.

The site where Abraham prepared to sacrifice Isaac, Mount Moriah, is traditionally connected with the Temple Mount in Jerusalem. Today, Mount Moriah is occupied by the Muslim shrine known as "the Dome of the Rock." A mere quarter of a mile from there is the

---

[82] Gen. 22:14.

place where it is believed Jesus was crucified. There *Yahweh-Yireh* provided the ultimate sacrifice that would bring eternal life to all who accept Jesus as their savior.

In Genesis, Abraham was prepared to sacrifice his only son, but Isaac was saved by God's miraculous provision. In the book of John, God's only Son is sacrificed as the miraculous provision for all people.

"For God so loved the world, that he gave his one and only Son, that whoever believes in him should not perish, but have eternal life." [83]

The same God whose love shines in the brilliance of wildflowers and who cares for each baby sparrow, sent His Son as the atoning sacrifice for our sins. [84] Jesus was the last and final sacrifice, the flawless lamb able to redeem all humanity and pay for the totality of our sins. Jesus is God's perfect and complete provision, the answer to our inmost concerns and the fulfillment of our deepest needs.

In Jesus' teaching we see one side of God's provision. In Jesus' mission on earth, we see another. Jesus came so that we might have life and have it in abundance. [85] This provision, this inestimable gift of

---

[83] John 3:16 (WEB).
[84] See Rom. 3:25.
[85] See John 10:10.

God's son, was a rescue, a ransom, a debt paid and a punishment borne for the most culpable and incapable among us. God's greatest act of provision came in the sacrifice of Jesus Christ. He provided a way of salvation for us because we couldn't do it on our own.

Occasionally God tests our hearts like He did Abraham's. He wants to know what we're willing to give up and sacrifice for Him before He opens the doors of provision and blessing.

What is it that you love more than anything else? What are your dreams? Will you follow Abraham's commitment to eagerly lay down those most precious possessions on the alter and willingly leave them all to follow Jesus? Instead of striving and fretting, will you trust Him to see ahead and provide what He knows you need?

It is marvelous to comprehend that God will not leave us in our sinful condition. He has provided a way out. His plan from the beginning was to provide a sacrificial lamb in Jesus. *Yahweh Yireh*, the God who provides, has presented a plan of salvation for us.

He deserves all our love and praise for that act alone.

Chapter Six

Shades of Ēl-Shaddai

Many Christians use the divine name *Ēl-Shaddai* in worship, but few of them understand its true meaning. Amy Grant popularized the song "El Shaddai" written by Michael Card and John Thompson. The lyrics magnified God Almighty—the wonderful *Ēl-Shaddai*. But what does *shaddai* actually mean, and what is the message and characteristic of God that is revealed to us in this powerful name?

We discover *Ēl-Shaddai* throughout the years of the Patriarchs, primarily when God appears to Abraham as God Almighty.

"When Abram was ninety-nine years old, the Lord appeared to him and said, "I am the Almighty God (*Ēl-Shaddai*); walk before me, and be thou perfect.

"And I will make my covenant between me and thee and will multiply thee exceedingly." [86]

Ēl-Shaddai is one of the many names of the God of the Old Testament. The divine name *Shaddai* appears forty-eight times in the Hebrew Bible, (seven times as *Ēl-Shaddai* and 41 times simply as *Shaddai*), but there is extensive debate surrounding the meaning of the word *Shaddai.* The various interpretations present shades of meaning that shed greater insight into the nature and characteristics of this God of the Old Testament.

Scholars seeking to understand the meaning of *Ēl-Shaddai* generally translate it as "God Almighty," the name used in several English translations of the Bible. [87]

For most Christians, *Ēl-Shaddai* means "God Almighty." In a world where we encounter daily struggles, we find refuge and rest in the shade of His strength. When we feel unsafe or uncertain in circumstances surrounding us, God's name, *Ēl-Shaddai*, reminds us that He is all-powerful, the Mighty One. In times of danger, He is the 9-1-1 emergency line we can call on. Psalm 91:1 assures us:

---

[86] Gen. 17:1, 2 (KJV).
[87] See Genesis 17:1 (NRSV, NIV, ESV).

"Whoever dwells in the shelter of the Most High will rest in the shadow of the Almighty." [88]

The most obvious expression of God's might is as the Creator. He is the Maker of all things in the universe.

"All things were created by Him, and apart from Him not one thing was created that has been created." [89]

Paul explains that "the builder of all things is God." [90]

Ēl-Shaddai is the God who sees and knows all. He has the power to go before us, to walk beside us and to protect us from behind. Living in God's presence gives us shelter and rest.

However, the traditional rendering "God Almighty" is highly debated and does not actually provide the basis for an accurate understanding of the meaning of *Ēl-Shaddai*.

The translators who worked on the Greek translation of the Old Testament, the Septuagint, did not understand the meaning imbedded in the name, *Ēl-Shaddai*. They translated it several different ways. In

---

[88] Psa. 91:1 (NIV).
[89] John 1:3.
[90] Heb. 3:4.

the book of Job, for instance, they translated *Shaddai* as *pantokratōr* or "The Ruler of All." Some interpret *shaddai* as "sufficient," and God as the "All-sufficient One." Gustave Oehler believed that early interpreters linked *Shaddai* to the Hebrew words *še* and *day*, translating the name *Ēl-Shaddai* as "He Who Is Sufficient." [91]

Either of these three interpretations describe God accurately because He is the all-sufficient mighty ruler of all. His provision can meet all our needs. His power sustains, nourishes and protects us. He takes our weakness and gives us His strength. He takes our inadequacies and, in His sufficiency, uses them to accomplish His great and powerful purposes.

This coincides with another suggested meaning for *Ēl-Shaddai* as "The Overpowerer," implying that God will do what He proposes to do, overpowering all opposition. Other translators associate *Ēl-Shaddai* with the Hebrew word *šadād*, meaning "destruction." The book of Joel 1:15 mentions "the destruction from *Shaddai*." [92] Tryggve Mettinger believes, however, that

---

[91] Oehler, Gustave F., *Theology of the Old Testament*. Zondervan Publishing House, p. 90.
[92] Joel 1:15.

this connotation "is probably a pun, not a linguistic historical derivation." [93]

There is a consensus among certain scholars that *shaddai* can be traced, not to Hebrew, but to an Accadian word meaning "mountain." In his article, *The Names Shaddai and Abraham,* [94] William Albright suggests that the root of *shaddai* comes from the Accadian *šadû,* or *shaddu,* meaning "mountain" and that expression produces the meaning, "The God of the Mountain."

"God came from Teman, and the Holy One from mount Paran. *Selah.* His glory covered the heavens, and the earth was full of his praise." [95]

In this verse, God is *Eloah*, meaning Deity. Teman was an Edomite city [96] named after a grandson of Esau. Mount Paran is located in the Sinai Peninsula.

""And he said, The LORD came from Sinai,...he shined forth from mount Paran." [97]

Both settings refer to the site where God displayed His mighty power in bringing Israel into the

---

[93] Mettinger, Tryggve N. D., *In Search of God: The Meaning and Message of the Everlasting Names.* Fortress Press, 1988, p. 70.

[94] Albright, William F., *The Names Shaddai and Abraham,* Journal of Biblical Literature 54 (1935): 173-204.

[95] Hab. 3:3.

[96] See Amos 1:12; Oba. 9.

[97] Duet. 33:2.

land of Canaan. [98] God's presence on that mountain surely reminded the Israelites of His power and provision. The God of the Mountain was the same God who mightily led His people from Egypt and appeared to them as a cloud by day and a fire at night.

The statement "God came from Teman" refers to God appearing on Mount Sinai to make covenants with His people. *Selah*, an expression used many times in the Psalms, means pause and consider what you just heard.

Habakkuk's prayer indicates that God is Lord and Ruler of all the earth. "Holy One" also refers to God, who is all-powerful. The glory of God fills the heavens and the earth. There is no glory greater than the glory of God in the heavens.

Ēl-Shaddai as the God of the Mountain could underscore God's invincible power or simply point to his symbolic abode. Mountain may also mean "holy place" or "temple." *Ēl-Shaddai* may also equate to the God of Israel known as "The Rock."

"As for the Rock, his work is perfect, for all his ways are just. He is a reliable God who is never unjust, he is fair and upright." [99]

---

[98] See Deut. 33:2; Jud. 5:4.
[99] Duet. 32:4.

Shaddai commonly appears in the Bible in the context of promises and blessings. *Ēl-Shaddai* appeared to Abraham and promised him that he would "be the father of a multitude of nations." [100] *Shaddai* blessed Sarah, promising that she would conceive a son in her old age. [101] *Shaddai* promised to bless Ishmael. [102]

Isaac blessed Jacob with the promise that he would become the father of many people: "*Ēl-Shaddai* bless you and make you fruitful and multiply you, that you may become a company of peoples." [103]

Ēl-Shaddai exhorted Jacob to be fruitful and multiply: "I am *Ēl-Shaddai*: be fruitful and multiply; a nation and a company of nations shall come from you, and kings shall spring from you." [104]

Job also recognized that *Shaddai* was the one who had blessed him with wealth, health, and children. [105] Naomi complained that *Shaddai* had taken away the blessings He had previously given to her. [106]

---

[100] Gen. 17:4 (NIV).
[101] Gen. 17:16 (NIV).
[102] Gen. 17:20 (NIV).
[103] Gen. 28:3.
[104] Gen. 35:11.
[105] Job 29:5.
[106] Ruth 1:20, 21.

It seems that after God revealed his name *Yahweh* to Moses, the name *Ēl-Shaddai* fell into disuse by the people of Israel. Moses proclaimed *Yahweh* as the true God, the God who had appeared to their fathers as *Ēl-Shaddai*. *Ēl-Shaddai* was the God of promise; *Yahweh* was the God about to fulfill all those promises.

The proclamation of God's power has mostly gone silent today. A God of love is more palpable and more easily received than the God who is sovereign and powerful—the Mighty God who can turn the hearts of governments and direct nations to do His will.

Habakkuk [107] recounts the Lord's mighty character, His anger over sin, and His authority over the nations. When God's prophets spoke His words, some listened and believed; others resisted. It is the same today when we speak of His power and might.

We should see God as He is: the reigning Lord God Almighty who will someday exercise His great power and reign forever. He is the God who chooses to make us holy, transforming our natures with His power. His name should be honored with reverence and awe. As the Psalmist says:

---

[107] Hab. 3:1-16.

"Be exalted, O LORD, in your strength! We will sing and praise your power."

We serve a mighty God, and we should honor his holy name. The Lord fed thousands from simple provisions. He healed the sick and worked mighty miracles to rescue His people. He urges us to call on Him so that He can show us great and mighty miracles. He is our solid rock, our deliverer, and our protector. We should love and trust Him with all our heart, soul, and mind.

The Lord calls, "Come unto me," because His power and provision will lead to peace. Someday we will witness the Mighty God of Isaiah [108] return with power and great glory. He whose name is above all names will be honored throughout eternity for the mercy He extends to us. All creation will ascribe to Him glory, majesty, power, and authority—the praise that *Ēl-Shaddai* deserves forevermore.

---

[108] See Isa. 9.

Chapter Seven

My Foundation, Adonai

The word *Adonai* is translated as "Lord" or "My Lord." The name *Adonai* literally means "My Foundation" and, by implication, "My Lord." It used to refer to any person "having power, authority, or influence; a master or ruler."

It is more accurate to say that *Adonai* by itself is not really a proper name but rather a title or appellative. It is translated as mister or my lord, master, or owner. David addresses God as *Adonai* and also uses the term *Adonai* to refer to Saul as "my lord the king." Abner refers to David in the same way. [109] Throughout the second book of Samuel, *Adonai* is used as a reference

---

[109] See 2 Sam. 3:21.

to David. Additionally, Elisha's followers use the term *Adonai* when referring to Elisha. [110]

Similarly, we today address Jesus as Lord but may also refer to the English poet George Gordon as "Lord Byron." Throughout the Old Testament we see the term *Adonai* used simply as a title of respect much in keeping with the English definition and usage of the word "lord."

Adonai is found over four hundred times in the Bible, and its meaning is revelatory in nature. *Adonai* is a form of the word *adon* from a root word meaning "to rule". *Adon* translates as lord, master, or ruler. It contains the concepts of dominion, rulership, and ownership. It is certainly a fitting title for God. While there are other lords who hold sway over limited realms, God is the Lord of all the earth. [111]

"O, Lord God [*Adonai*], you have begun to show me your greatness and strength. (What god in heaven or earth can rival your works and mighty deeds?)" [112]

The cultural background to the word *adon* deals with governing authorities such as kings, [113] military

---

[110] See 2 Kings 2:19.
[111] See Josh. 3:11.
[112] Duet. 3:24.
[113] See Dan. 1:10.

commanders, [114] teachers and mentors, [115] and even older brothers. [116] It was also used for employers and owners of servants and slaves. [117] The title *Adon* likewise bore within it a certain responsibility for the care and well-being of that which was owned. The master was to provide for, protect, guide, and boost that which he owned.

The verb אדן *('dn)* means "to provide support for a piece of superstructure: to be a base for something big to stand or rotate upon." The noun אדן *('eden)* refers to "the foundation, base or pedestal of pillars or panels" and such, and this word is lavishly featured in the description of the tabernacle, a prototype of the temple. The bases and foundations of the temple characterized the foundation known as אדון *('adon)* translated as lord, sir, or mister.

The word *Adonai* comes from the root אדן *('dn)* and its true meaning is disputed. The BDB Theological Dictionary lists the following proposals: *Adonai* is comparable to the Assyrian word *adannu,* meaning firm or strong, and the associated adverb *adannis* meaning strongly or exceedingly. Or, it may have to do with a Persian word meaning firm or fasten, therefore

---

[114] See 2 Kings 5:1.
[115] See 2 Kings 6:5.
[116] See Gen. 32:4.
[117] See Gen. 24:65.

meaning to determine, consequently to command, or to rule. Some suggest a relationship to an Arabic verb that means to be obedient or cause obedience, and consequently to govern and rule.

The term *Adonai* hints at the notion of ownership and being the steward of what is owned. When God is referred to as *Adonai*, He is alluded to as Owner. This is illustrated in numerous Bible passages that show God not only as our master, but as our protector and provider as well.

"However, fear the Lord and serve him faithfully with all your heart. Just look at the great things he has done for you!" [118]

The psalmist wrote that God is, "the (*Adonai*) of the whole earth." [119] He is not merely the Creator (*Ēlohim*), but He is also the Owner (*Adonai*). God reveals this ownership in Scripture: "For every beast of the forest is Mine, the cattle on a thousand hills." [120]

In Biblical times, masters had a responsibility to protect, provide for, and promote their servants to earned positions of authority. Psalm 123:2 illustrates the positive relationship between master and servant:

---

[118] 1 Sam. 12:24.
[119] See Psa. 97.
[120] Psa. 50:10 (NIV).

"Behold, as the eyes of servants look to the hand of their master, as the eyes of a maidservant to the hand of her mistress, so our eyes look to the LORD our God, till he has mercy upon us." [121]

There are many examples where *Adonai* is shown to be a gracious master. The verse from Psalm 86 shows that God is willing to be a gracious and loving master to all who call upon Him:

"Certainly, O Lord [*Adonai*], you are kind and forgiving, and show great faithfulness to all who cry out to you." [122]

We are all invited into this relationship of having God as our own personal lord and master and to experience the benefits of serving Him as *Adonai*.

Adonai is also the source of the name Jehovah. During the Hellenistic period (approximately 323 BC to 31 AD), the Jews observed the tradition of not pronouncing *YHWH* because it was considered too sacred a word. When the Masoretes wanted to preserve the pronunciation of the words used in the Bible they came upon a problem. *YHWH* was the original form of God's name. It was revered to the point of not even being pronounced. To circumvent the

---

[121] Other translations read: "until He shows us favor" (HCSB) or "until He is gracious to us" (NASB).
[122] Psa. 86:5.

problem, the Masoretes inserted the vowel symbols that go with *Adonai*, indicating that whenever readers saw *YHWH*, they were to say *Adonai*. Even today, when reading the Hebrew text, the Israelites will pronounce *YHWH* as *Adonai*.

In the English language Bible, it is necessary to differentiate between the words "Lord" and "LORD." Every time the word "Lord" is used in the Bible, the Hebrew behind the word is *Adonai*. Every time the word "LORD" is used, the Hebrew behind the word is *YHWH*.

Adonai, as the definition states, has a possessive quality to it. In Exodus, God calls Moses to declare His name to Pharaoh so that Pharaoh would know that God was claiming the Hebrews as His own people.

"You picked them out of all the nations of the earth to be your special possession, just as you, O sovereign Lord, announced through your servant Moses when you brought our ancestors out of Egypt." [123]

Adonai also describes the God who demands justice for His people. The prophet Isaiah saw in vision the upcoming punishment for the King of Assyria for his acts against Israel.

---

[123] 1 Kings 8:53.

"Therefore, the Lord, the Lord Almighty, will send a wasting disease upon his sturdy warriors; under his pomp a fire will be kindled like a blazing flame." [124]

Adonai also conveys the sound of praise. King David rejoiced in acknowledging God's authority, and proudly declared it:

"Lord, our Lord, how majestic is your name in all the earth! You have set your glory in the heavens." [125]

"Give thanks to the Lord of lords, for his loyal love endures." [126]

Since God is the absolute ruler and owner, our devotion to Him as *Adonai* is demonstrated through surrender and submission. The concept of being owned may conjure images of one person possessing another but slavery has no place in our world. The concept of *Adonai* is not about oppression, but about God's position of leadership in our lives. The Hebrews saw themselves as autonomous agents in the Creator's activities and not as blindly obedient slaves or lifeless pawns controlled at the will and whim of a despot God. Submission can be very powerful when coupled with an Omnipotent God.

---

[124] Isa. 10:16 (NIV).
[125] Psalm 8:1 (NIV).
[126] Psa. 136:3.

One truth in life is that everyone will eventually serve someone, but we have a choice in who that will be. The Scriptures clearly state that God is always present and that He is rightfully Lord over all. We can submit to Him as a child to a good Father. Imagine serving a master who returns your loyalty with unconditional love, comfort, and abundant provision. The loving Lordship that God offers is a humbling and glorious experience.

To fully appreciate the Lord as *Adonai* we must accept God as ruler, master, and owner over our lives. To experience all that God can do for us, we must knowingly and willingly surrender to Him. We need to let Him call the shots and have the final say in all our important decisions.

The word *Adonai* reminds us of the position and status God desires to obtain in our lives. He calls for our submission, not as a harsh master over us, but as our loving King. He requires our obedience solely so He can fill our lives with blessings.

The title *Adonai* is a gift from God to His people, a reassuring reminder of who is in control. The more we acknowledge Him as *Adonai*, the more we will see of His goodness. When we allow Him to correct us, we will grow in wisdom. As we surrender to His rule, we will experience more joy and peace in serving Him. Allowing God to be our Master draws us closer to Him.

"You are the Lord; my only source of well-being." [127]

Jesus Christ is the King of kings and the Lord of lords. He reigns forever. He is our Savior, our Redeemer, and our God. We can find salvation in Him and Him alone. [128] Surrender to God and honor Him as *Adonai* and watch the heavens unfold His glorious plan for your life.

---

[127] Psa. 16:2.
[128] Gen. 15:2; Jud. 6:15; Mal. 1:6; Deut. 10:17; Psa. 2:4, 8:1, 97:5, 136:3; Isa. 1:24, 6:1; Rom. 10:9.

Chapter Eight

Look to Jehovah Nissi

Exodus 17 relates a riveting narrative. God had just rescued the Israelites from generations of slavery in Egypt. He brought them through the Red Sea and into the wilderness. The Israelites wandered in the desert after leaving Egypt. Along the way, they were suddenly attacked by a hostile band of powerful and warlike nomads known as the Amalekites. In a rather unexpected way, God grants them victory.

When Israel faced the Amalekites in battle at Rephidim it wasn't with an experienced army, the best commanders or overwhelming military strength. They were a transient tribe of herdsmen escaping slavery, travelling with utter uncertainty toward a promised land they hadn't been to in over four hundred years. They were trespassers in a territory of fierce fighting inhabitants. They travelled with women, children, herds, and all their possessions. Their battle was for survival and for a future in the land God had given them.

But they travelled with something that no other nation on earth had—a pillar of fire, a cloud of smoke, and the very presence of God. Israel would not fight this battle alone. No matter how inexperienced or overmatched, they were not the underdogs. No matter how desperate or overwhelmed they felt, they were never at a loss. The most powerful commander and the perfect protector, Jehovah *Nissi*, was with them. (Jehovah *Nissi* is from the King James Bible. The Hebrew is pronounced *Yahweh Nissi*.)

As the battle commenced, Moses stood on top of a hill where he could see the armies below him. He held in his hand the "rod of God"—the same rod with which he had struck a rock to bring forth water for the people in the desert. [129] As the armies lined up to do battle, the men of Israel, under the command of their newly appointed general, Joshua, could look up to that nearby peak and see three individuals—Moses, Aaron, and Hur—overlooking the battlefield.

---

[129] See Exo.17:5, 6.

The battle was definitely an unusual one. When the first battle cry sounded and the foes engaged, Moses, standing between Aaron and Hur, raised his hands over the battle, and as he did, Israel began to take the upper hand.

"As long as Moses held up his hands, the Israelites were winning, but whenever he lowered his hands, the Amalekites were winning." [130]

As the battle wore on, the sun rose high and hot. Moses wearied and his arms dropped to his side. "The spirit is willing,' the gospel of Mark tells us, "but the flesh is weak." [131] Immediately, the Amalekites galvanized and began to impinge upon the Israelites. Aaron and Hur realized what was taking place. They dragged over a small boulder for Moses to sit on and they each took one of Moses' arms and raised them again over the battle. As they did this, the Israelite fighters rallied to Joshua, found new strength, and the Amalekites cowered in renewed fear.

Throughout the rest of the afternoon and into the evening, Aaron and Hur supported Moses' arms and the rod-like banners in the time of battle and God supported the Israelites. As soldiers fight under the flag that bear the insignia of their country, the Israelites

---

[130] Exo. 17:11.
[131] Mark 14:38.

fought under the direction of Jehovah-*Nissi*. Under His banner they rallied, with His aid they fought, and in His name they prevailed and conquered.

By sunset, Israel had defeated the Amalekites. [132] This was a significant and memorable day for the Israelite nation because it was the day God first showed them that He fought for them and that He protected and conquered on their behalf. Following the battle, Moses built an altar and named it: *Yahweh Nissi*—the Lord is my banner. [133]

"The battle is the Lord's," wrote the prophet Samuel. [134] The unique manner in which Israel prevailed left no doubt who was responsible for their glorious victory. Only as the rod of God was held aloft did the Israelites conquer. The battle was not won with overwhelming military might, it was not won through superior strategic battle plans; it was won by the power of God.

Yahweh Nissi means "The Lord is my banner." This name of God distinguishes Him as our defense, our director, and our deliverer. The same divine deliverance and protection the Lord provided for the Israelites against their enemies is equally offered to us today from the enemies we face in life. Naming the altar

---

[132] Exo. 17:12, 13.
[133] See Exo. 17:15.
[134] Sam. 17:47.

Jehovah-*Nissi* serves as a reminder to believers of every age and era that we can be victorious as we honor the name of the Lord and rally to Him as our banner. As the Psalmist wrote: "You have given a banner to those who fear you, that it may be displayed because of the truth." [135]

The name Jehovah-*Nissi* appears only once in the Bible, but it is one of many descriptive names for God. The name Jehovah-*Nissi* gives us great hope. It represents the allegiance between God and His people. He pledges to protect us; we pledge to follow Him.

The names ascribed to God in the Bible always give us insight into His character. To better comprehend God's nature, we must understand what His names signify. The Hebrew root word *nes* appears several times throughout the Old Testament. It describes a pole supporting a standard or an ensign.

The word *nes* often refers to Jesus. In Numbers, Chapter 21, when the plague-struck Israelites were dying, Moses attached a bronze serpent to a pole (*nes*) and set it up for the people to see. Those who looked at the bronze serpent were healed. The New Testament ties that incident to Jesus, who was raised up on the

---

[135] Psalm 60:4.

cross so that everyone who looks to Him will be saved.[136]

Isaiah also uses *nes* to speak prophetically of Jesus:

"At that time a root from Jesse will stand like a signal flag (*nes*) for the nations. Nations will look to him for guidance, and his residence will be majestic.

"At that time the sovereign master will again lift his hand to reclaim the remnant of his people...

"He will lift a signal flag (*nes*) for the nations; he will gather Israel's dispersed people and assemble Judah's scattered people from the four corners of the earth." [137]

In this context, the word *nes* or "banner" should be familiar to us today; an enormous sign meant to be seen by everyone. More specifically, it is a sign meant to give confidence, encouragement and hope to a particular group or team.

Armies raise the banner of their country during a war to spur them on in battle. It provides motivation to fight and conquer. In the battle with the Amalekites, the Israelites looked to God—not man—for deliverance. They rallied to God, and He made them victorious.

---

[136] John 3:14; Phil. 2:9.
[137] Isa. 11:10-12.

"For the Lord your God goes with you to fight on your behalf against your enemies to give you victory." [138]

The image of the character of God portrayed by Moses' declaration *Yahweh Nissi* is that God is the banner for all those who believe in Him, follow Him, and trust Him with the same faith demonstrated by Moses, Aaron, Hur, and Joshua.

Banners are raised to remember, celebrate, announce and honor. We hang them in arenas to honor champions. We raise them to honor soldiers returning from war. We display banners on holidays to commemorate important, meaningful dates. Banners display names or images we can easily recognize from far off. They mark a location to rally around, or they identify a business or event so we can better locate it. When Moses built the altar and called it, "The LORD is my banner," he was creating a seat of honor, a place of remembrance, a celebration of victory, an expression of gratitude.

Banners must be visible. Their purpose is to be seen, noticeable and unmistakable. They are an invitation and a summons. They call out to wanderers.

---

[138] Deut. 20:4.

God becomes our banner when we celebrate and honor His faithfulness to us. He becomes our banner when we remember the support He so freely gives us. He becomes our banner when we identify ourselves as His children. God becomes our banner when we become His representatives making Him visible to the world. He becomes our banner when we respond to His invitation and summons to follow Jesus.

The Lord gives us victory in spiritual warfare. When the enemy attacks, the Lord raises the banner of His love over us. He wages war against all evil forces on our behalf and makes us conquerors in Christ. [139]

We may not be at war with enemy soldiers, but we can often find ourselves under spiritual attack. We may be battling with temptation. We may be battling anxiety. We may be wrestling with the seeds of doubt that the world plants in our hearts and minds. We may be fighting just to make it through another difficult day on our own. We get weary, upset and angry, and sometimes we end up losing control. In all those battles, we can rally to the Lord who is our banner.

Like our personal banner, God goes with us into battle and helps us to overcome our enemies. Victory does not come from our own strength, but from His divine power.

---

[139] Exo. 17:15.

Jehovah-*Nissi* can be the one we look to in our time of need. When the battle seems lost, God's name is a reminder to all that He is our banner, our deliverer and our protector. He alone is able to lead us and give us spiritual victory over the problems and impediments that come our way. If we allow Him, He will do more on our behalf than we could ever do on our own.

"I look up toward the hills. From where does my help come? My help comes from the Lord, the Creator of heaven and earth." [140]

---

[140] Psa. 121:1, 2.

Chapter Nine

Ēl-'Elyon, the Most High

Glance at a newspaper or turn on the TV news and the entire world appears to be in a constant state of chaos and confusion. Earthquakes, hurricanes, fires and floods, out of control viruses, domestic violence, rogue nations going to war, marriages casually tossed aside, financial distresses and so many other occurrences may leave us to wonder if anyone is in control of our world.

Someone most assuredly is! *Ēl-'Elyon* is in complete control. Nothing takes Him by surprise. He isn't blindsided by wars, diseases, or politics. *Ēl-'Elyon* – the Most High God—is the sovereign ruler of the universe.

Ēl-'Elyon is one of the truly exquisite names for God. *Ēl-Elyon* reveals that God is above all gods, that nothing in life is more sacred. He is the Lord Most High who reigns supreme. He is greater than any force of darkness and bigger than any problem we could ever face in life.

The name *Ēl-'Elyon* is translated as "the Most High God." [141] The Hebrew word *Ēl* used alone means God Most High. *Ēl* is a shortened form of *Ēlohim* and conveys God's strength. *Elyon* is the superlative form of *Ēl* and is interpreted as "the strongest." The combination of *Ēl* and *Elyon* creates a powerful name which means "the Extremely-Exalted, Sovereign, High God."

"I cry out to the Most High *Ēl*ohim, To *Ēl* who is perfecting all matters for me." [142]

The word *'Elyon* is an adjective derived from the Hebrew root *'lh*, which means to "go up" or "ascend." Spatially, the adjective denotes the highest or uppermost.

It is used to designate height: "Nevertheless, the high places [*'elyon*] were not removed. The people still sacrificed and made offerings on the high places [*'elyon*]. He built the upper gate of the house of the LORD." [143]

---

[141] See Gen.14:18-22.
[142] Psa. 57:2.
[143] 2 Kings 15:35 (ESV).

It defines the stature of individuals: "I will also appoint him my firstborn, the highest ['elyon] of the kings of the earth." [144]

It declares the prominence of Israel: "So as to set you high above ['elyon] all nations which He has made, for a praise, and for a name, and for esteem, and for you to be a set-apart people." [145]

In reference to God, the compound is construed as a name: "It is good to make music to your name, O Most High." [146] Closely linked to temple services, Ēl-'Elyon denotes exaltation and absolute lordship.

Ēl-'Elyon is infinite in power. He has demonstrated that power in the work of creation where his mere word of command brought the world into existence and gave it order. [147] Ēl-'Elyon, therefore, is the strongest strong One, or "the most high God."

He is the "possessor of heaven and earth." [148] His authority transcends the boundaries between nations, between Heaven and earth, between spiritual and physical beings, and between angels and demons. His authority and dominion span time and distance.

---

[144] Psa. 89:27.
[145] Deut. 26:19.
[146] Psa. 9:1.
[147] See Gen. 1:3.
[148] Gen. 14:19.

Nothing and no one within this infinite universe fall outside of His domain and jurisdiction.

Abram Encounters Ēl-'Elyon.

Abram encountered the Most High God after rescuing his nephew, Lot. As Abram was returning home, he met Melchizedek who introduced himself as the king of Salem and priest of God Most High [Ēl-'Elyon]. "Melchizedek, king of Salem, brought forth bread and wine; and he was the priest of the most high God." [149]

The other kings Abram had met were all worshippers of Canaanite gods. Melchizedek made it clear that he represented the Ēl-'Elyon, Most High God. "Blessed be Abram of God Most High, possessor of heaven and earth; and blessed be God Most High who has delivered your enemies into your hand." [150]

Abraham had made enemies of the four kings from the east. He had humiliated them in the rescue of Lot. He had also alienated the king of Sodom by pledging allegiance to Ēl-'Elyon and refusing any of the spoils of war. Ēl-'Elyon, the Most High God is the reason given by Melchizedek for Abram's victory over a much larger and superior force. Abram, in turn, pledged

---

[149] Gen. 14:18.
[150] Gen. 14:19, 20 (NKJV).

allegiance to "the most high God, the possessor of heaven and earth." [151]

"After these things the word of the LORD came to Abram in a vision: 'Fear not, Abram, I am your shield; your reward shall be very great.'" [152]

This could be considered the ultimate life insurance policy and the best pension plan ever! The strongest strong One, the Most High God, would protect Abraham (I am your shield). *Ēl-'Elyon*, the possessor of Heaven and earth, the one who owns the cattle on a thousand hills, would be his "very great" great reward.

Moses Writes of *Ēl-'Elyon*

Moses was nearing the end of his mortal life when God commanded him to write a song as a reminder to Israel of who God is. The song should address God's faithfulness, His sovereignty, and His salvation. It should stand as a witness to all Israel that the evils, suffering and sorrow that would befall them throughout time were not to be blamed on God but would be, instead, the result of their own unfaithfulness and sin.

---

[151] Gen. 14:22.
[152] Gen. 15:1 (ESV).

God commanded Moses: "Now, therefore, write this song for you, and teach it to the children of Israel; put it in their mouths, that this song may be a witness for me against the children of Israel." [153]

Moses then composed these words: "When the Most High [*'Elyon*] divided to the nations their inheritance, when he separated the sons of Adam, he set the bounds of the people according to the number of the children of Israel. For the Lord's portion is his people; Jacob is the lot of his inheritance." [154]

'Elyon, the possessor of Heaven and earth, with sovereign authority, partitioned off this planet. As God's inheritance, Israel is the hub of the earth. [155] He set the boundaries of the nations regarding the little land of Israel. Jerusalem will become God's home and His ensign will fly over Zion.

Nebuchadnezzar meets *Ēl-'Elyon*

Nebuchadnezzar, king of Babylon, dreamed of a great image of a man. Its head was gold, its breast and arms were silver, its belly and thighs were brass, its legs were iron, and its feet were a mixture of iron and clay.

---

[153] Duet. 31:19
[154] Duet. 32:8, 9.
[155] Ezek. 38:12.

[156] The value of the metals decreased from head to toe but their strength increased. Silver is stronger than gold; brass is stronger than silver; and iron is stronger than brass.

This image depicts four great Gentile empires—Babylon, Medo-Persia, Greece and Rome—all of whom would impact Israel, beginning with the Babylonian captivity of Judah in 606 B.C. and ending with the literal return of Christ to Jerusalem. It was foretold that "Jerusalem shall be trodden down by the Gentiles, until the times of the Gentiles be fulfilled" [157] and that no descendant of Abraham, [158] of the tribe of Judah [159] or of the family of David [160] would prosper in ruling Israel.

Nebuchadnezzar is revealed by Daniel as the head of gold: "Thou, O king, art a king of kings; for the God of heaven [*'Elyon*] hath given thee a kingdom, power, and strength, and glory. And wherever the children of men dwell, the beasts of the field and the fowls of the heavens hath he given into thine hand, and hath made thee ruler over them all. Thou art this head of gold." [161]

---

[156] See Dan. 2:31-33.
[157] Luke 21:24.
[158] Gen. 12:7.
[159] Gen. 49:10.
[160] 2 Sam. 7:12, 13.
[161] Dan. 2:37, 38 (KJV).

Nebuchadnezzar was an absolute ruler empowered under divine authorization and he did a spectacular job of exalting himself over a pagan kingdom, but Nebuchadnezzar exceeded his authority. He was lifted up with self-importance. "The king spoke, and said, Is not this great Babylon, that I have built for the house of the kingdom by the might of my power, and for the honor of my majesty?" [162]

Then one day God tired of Nebuchadnezzar's boasting. The Prophet Daniel had warned the king in the name of *'Elyon* (the Most High) that he would go insane for seven years ". . . till thou know that the Most High ruleth in the kingdom of men, and giveth it to whomsoever he will." [163] Daniel counseled the king to repent of his pride, to break off his sins and to show mercy to the poor [164] but there was no repentance.

As foretold, Nebuchadnezzar, the head of gold of the Gentile world powers, went insane, living and acting like a wild animal for seven years. [165] Because he exalted himself above God, Nebuchadnezzar's pride precipitously drove him from palace to pasture and from ruler to ruins.

---

[162] Dan. 4:30.
[163] Dan 4:25.
[164] Dan. 4:27.
[165] Dan. 4:33.

Eventually realizing that he was nothing compared to the sovereign God, Nebuchadnezzar came to his senses:

"At the end of the time I, Nebuchadnezzar, lifted my eyes to heaven, and my understanding returned to me; and I blessed the Most High and praised and honored Him who lives forever." [166]

Nebuchadnezzar believed he was great and powerful until He met Ēl-'Elyon and finally came to understand what refined, advanced, modern twentieth-century civilization has yet to realize—that the God of creation, Ēl-'Elyon, the Most High God, is the strongest strong One, the possessor of Heaven and earth. No one and nothing can resist His will.

The Lord Most High calls His people into faithful service. We are stewards entrusted with the Master's possessions, charged to do His will for His glory and our good. Even if we are masters of one kind or another on earth, we must remember that we also have a Master in heaven. [167] Our greatest wisdom is to obey the commands of the Most High and to be faithfully focused on serving Him.

---

[166] Dan. 4:34 (NKJV).
[167] See Eph. 6:9.

The Ark and *Ēl-'Elyon*

The account of the Philistines capturing the Ark of the Covenant helps us appreciate and understand that *Ēl-'Elyon* is God Most High. After the Philistines had seized the Ark of the Covenant, they set it beside their own idol, Dagon. The following day Dagon fell over, bowing before the Lord Most High. The Philistines lifted Dagon up again and the next day their idol fell once more, breaking its head and hands. The Lord Most High demonstrated that no idol, ancient or modern, can replace Him.

Demons Know *Ēl-'Elyon*

The sphere of influence and control of *Ēl-'Elyon*, Most High God, the strongest strong One, the possessor of Heaven and earth, ranges far beyond the physical, earthly dominion and includes the unseen spirit realm. As Jesus crossed the Sea of Galilee into the land of the Gadarenes He encountered a man possessed by a demon whose name was Legion, indicating that the man was possessed by many demons. But the authority of *Ēl-'Elyon*, the God of Abraham, extends beyond the little land of Israel and encompasses even the entirety of the demonic world.

The demon, recognizing Jesus as the Son of God, "cried with a loud voice, and said, What have I to do with thee, Jesus, thou Son of the Most High God [*Ēl-'Elyon*]? I adjure thee by God, that thou torment me not." [168] Jesus commanded the demons to leave the man and enter a nearby herd of swine, and the herd ran down a steep incline into the sea and drowned. [169]

Lucifer versus *Ēl-'Elyon*

Another account where the name *Ēl-'Elyon* is used to identify God is when the prophet Isaiah recounts the dreadful fall of Lucifer from heaven. Before the advent of man, Lucifer, or Satan, the son of the morning, rebelled against his Creator. The Old Testament records this tragic event:

"How art thou fallen from heaven, O Lucifer, son of the morning! How art thou cut down to the ground, who didst weaken the nations! For thou hast said in thine heart, I will ascend into heaven, I will exalt my throne above the stars of God; I will sit also upon the mount of the congregation, in the sides of the north, I will ascend above the heights of the clouds, I will be like the Most High [*'Elyon*]." [170]

---

[168] Mark 5:7.

[169] See Mark 5:7-13.
[170] Isa. 14:12-14.

Satan, lifted up with pride, seeking to be like God, declares five "I will" statements: "I will ascend;" "I will exalt;" "I will sit;" "I will ascend:" And the final "I will" is that Satan will "be like the Most High." Did he not realize that there could be only one "Most High"—one strongest strong One? From the authentic Most High, Ēl-'Elyon, came the irrefutable and inescapable decree:

"Yet thou shall be brought down to sheol, to the sides of the pit." [171] Satan could never successfully prevail against the Most High God. From Satan's own mouth came the acknowledgement and witness of the sovereignty of God when he uttered the words "I will be like the Most High." Satan himself admits here that there is none higher than Ēl-'Elyon.

The triumphant truth behind all of this is that "greater is he [Jesus] that is in you, than he [Satan] that is in the world." [172]

---

[171] Isa. 14:15.
[172] 1 John 4:4.

Ēl-'Elyon: The Unknown God

In the New Testament, the Greek words *Theou hypistou* [173] are translated as Most High God. They describe the Lord as the highest possible object of worship. Human-made gods and idols cannot compete with the Lord and are not to be worshiped. [174]

During Paul's missionary journeys, certain philosophers brought him to the Areopagus at Athens and asked: "May we know what this new doctrine, of which thou speakest, is?" [175]

"Then Paul stood in the midst of Mars' Hill, and said, Ye men of Athens, I perceive that in all things ye are very religious. For as I passed by, and beheld your devotions, I found an altar with this inscription, TO THE UNKNOWN GOD." [176]

The Athenians were very religious. They built altars to their many gods and just in case there was a god they didn't know—one they had left out and possibly offended—they built an altar to this "unknown god." This presented a perfect teaching opportunity for Paul. Referring to their "unknown god" Paul declared:

---

[173] Luke 8:28; Heb. 7:1.
[174] See Deut. 27:13; Rev. 9:20.
[175] Acts 17:19.
[176] Acts 17:22, 23.

"Whom, therefore, ye ignorantly worship, him declare I unto you." [177]

Paul then identifies this God as the Lord of Heaven and earth (*Ēl-'Elyon*) who dwelleth not in temples made with hands [178] and the one who "made of one blood all nations of men to dwell on all the face of the earth, and hath determined the times before appointed, and the bounds of their habitation." [179] It is in the Most High God that men live, and move, and have their being. [180] In response to Paul's message, some of the citizens of Athens agreed to hear him out and some of them "joined him, and believed." [181]

God is sovereign and He is in absolute control. When the world appears as if no one is in command, we may be assured that *Ēl-'Elyon* has perfect charge of all that happens in this world. Our God, *Ēl-'Elyon*, is the Most High God, the strongest strong One, the possessor of Heaven and earth. Through our faith in the Lord Jesus Christ, we can stand resolute on the one immovable point in a constantly changing world, and that is that no one in this life is more secure than the loved ones of the Savior.

---

[177] Acts 17:23.
[178] See Acts 17:24.
[179] Acts 17:26.
[180] Acts 17:28.
[181] Acts 17:34.

God Most High invites all humanity to know Him. The fundamental and essential way to know God Most High is through knowing Jesus Christ.

Chapter Ten

Alpha and Omega

There is no great mystery hidden in the words "alpha and omega." Alpha and omega are the first and last letters of the Greek alphabet, the language used in writing the New Testament. Yet what does it mean that God is Alpha and Omega?

Among the Jewish rabbis, it was common to use the first and the last letters of the Hebrew alphabet to denote the whole of anything, from beginning to end. The respective positions of these letters illustrate that God (Jehovah) is the beginning and the end. [182] He was Almighty God in the infinite past, and he will continue

---

[182] Rev. 21:6.

to be Almighty God forever. He is the one who is "from everlasting to everlasting." [183]

Jehovah declares: "I am the first and I am the last. There is no God but me." [184] In this case, the expression "the first and the last" has the same meaning as "the Alpha and the Omega." Jehovah emphasizes that He is the everlasting true God; beside Him, there is no other. [185]

As finite humans, we understand beginnings and endings. We comprehend the cycles of our lives; that we are born, we live, and ultimately, that we will die physically. Our understanding of God is also often linear. The minute we speak of the infinite, diminishing and increasing cease to exist.

Jesus proclaimed Himself to be the "Alpha and Omega who is, and who was, and who is to come, the Almighty." [186] What a revelatory statement! The New Testament verse where Jesus proclaims that He is "the Alpha and the Omega, the First and the Last, the Beginning and the End" [187] is surely a reference to the one true God. Such a statement of eternality could apply only to God. The finite mind wrestles with such a

---

[183] Psa. 90:2.
[184] Isa. 44:6.
[185] Duet. 4:35, 39.
[186] Rev. 1:8.
[187] Rev. 22:13.

profound pronouncement. It is wonderous to comprehend that God was, is, and always will be.

Jesus is the "Alpha and Omega" in that He was at the beginning of all things and will be at the close. He always existed and always will exist. He has no beginning, nor will He have any end with respect to time, being from everlasting to everlasting. It was Christ who brought about the creation: "Through him all things were made; without him nothing was made that has been made." [188] His Second Coming will be the beginning of the end of creation as we know it. [189]

The Lord may also be designated as the Alpha and Omega in the sense of rank. He is Alpha, the first, the chief, the foremost, the Eternal God. Alpha was frequently used by the Hebrews to signify the best, just as we at one time were accustomed to use the letter A, as in "A1" or "A-okay."

Jesus is the "Alpha and Omega" in that He identifies Himself as the God of the Old Testament. Isaiah ascribes this aspect of Jesus' nature as part of the Godhead in several places:

"I, the Lord, am the first; and with the last I am He." [190]

---

[188] John 1:3.
[189] 2 Pet. 3:10.
[190] Isa. 41:4 (NKJV).

"I am the first, and I am the last; and beside me there is no God." [191]

"I am he; I am the first, I also am the last." [192]

These are clear indications of the eternal nature of the Godhead, and, in this sense, Jesus Christ is truly the Alpha, regardless of any other title ascribed to him. If we call him a prophet, then all the prophets follow at a humble distance, bearing witness of Him. When He sits upon His throne as king, then He is King of kings, and His dominion is an everlasting dominion, his kingdom is from generation to generation. If we refer to Him as the Great High Priest, then He is the fulfilment of all set forth by that priesthood title. If He is our shepherd, then He is the Great Shepherd who shall appear. As the cornerstone, He is the Chief Cornerstone. In all these respects, He is the Alpha, surpassing anything that may be compared to Him, as the sun outshines the stars, or as the sea exceeds a drop of heavenly dew.

Christ, as the Alpha and Omega, is the first and last in so many ways. He is the "author and finisher" of our faith, [193] signifying that He begins it and carries it through to completion. He is the sum and substance of

---

[191] Isa. 44:6.
[192] Isa. 48:12.
[193] See Heb. 12:2.

the Scriptures, both of the Law and of the Gospel. [194] He is revealed in the first verse of Genesis and disclosed in the last verse of Revelation. He is the fulfilling end of the Law [195] and He is the beginning of the gospel of grace. [196]

We should study the Bible in this light; considering it to be a window through which Christ looks down on us and then, we perusing its pages see His image in preparation for when we shall see Him face to face. The essence of the Word of God is Christ. Distilling its underlying quality we discover Jesus of Nazareth, the Son of God, and the King of the Jews, the Alpha and Omega of holy Scripture.

A. W. Tozer, author of the classic book, *The Pursuit of God*, wrote:

"If we grope back to the farthest limits of thought where imagination touches the pre-creation void, we shall find God there. In one unified present glance, He comprehends all things from everlasting, and the flutter of a seraph's wing a thousand ages hence is seen by Him now without moving His eyes."

As the works of God are enlarged and extended, as knowledge of the universe grows on every side,

---

[194] See John 1:1, 14.
[195] See Matt. 5:17.
[196] See Eph. 2:8, 9.

Christ is there still, bearing the name of Alpha and Omega.

Applying the Concept of Alpha to Our Lives

The Merriam-Webster Online Dictionary defines Alpha this way: Something that is first. Other words for Alpha include beginning, creation, and origination.

We all have our own "firsts." At conception, our life begins and continues in a linear fashion. We achieve many important milestones; we learn to walk, to talk, we grow and are educated, we marry and begin the cycle again. God endows our beginnings. He supports our new endeavors and can guide important decisions. He delights when we first call on Him for major decisions. When we turn the difficult decisions over to Him, when we seek His guidance first, we can know He is directing us towards what's best for our lives.

A divine plan was conceived before our earthly beginnings. God knew of us before our mothers ever held us—that is the beauty of God as Alpha. God is present in every new dawning day. We can call upon Him first thing every morning. We can ask for His blessings and protection.

Applying the Concept of Omega to Our Lives

The Merriam-Webster Online Dictionary defines Omega as: The extreme of the final part. Other words for Omega are the last, conclusion, and perfection.

God has the final word. We should invite Him into all our earthly matters and trust His perfect will. As we surrender our accomplishments and our disappointments, our downs as well as our ups, to Christ, we demonstrate trust in God's authority and power to handle every issue. Every situation in our lives can be under spiritual quality-control.

Beyond a doubt, Christ is the Alpha and Omega in all covenant transactions. Our earthly stories will end. The ups and downs, the difficult and easy, the exciting and the sorrowful, it doesn't matter—they will all end. When God is our Omega, we can look forward to a fortuitous future. We can trust His perfect will in every chapter of our lives. He is the Author and Finisher of our faith.

A magnificent finale is coming. "No eye has seen, no ear has heard, and no mind has imagined what God has prepared for those who love him." [197] An infinite future is imprinted on our hearts.

---

[197] 2 Cor. 2:9 (NLT).

On Patmos, God gave the Apostle John a vision of our future. "Then the one seated on the throne said, 'Look, I am making everything new...I am the Alpha and Omega, the beginning and the end...the one who conquers will inherit these things and I will be his God.'" [198] As Omega, God is preparing an ending permeated in divine majesty. Beyond earthly thrones, above social statuses, greater than political empowerment, what awaits us is unfathomable!

The first breath to escape the human lungs, the first light to greet the newly opened eye, comes from Jesus who is the Alpha; the final shout of faith, the last cry of joy and praise shall be for Him who is the Omega. The thoughts of God, the inscrutable purposes of Jehovah, His eternal decrees, these are deep subjects; but this we know: In all things from first to last, they relate to Christ. In eternity, heaven and earth shall adore Jesus Christ as Alpha and Omega.

Our Lord should be the beginning and the end of our life's design. May we continually bless the name of Alpha and Omega, the beginning and the end, the first and the last!

---

[198] Rev. 21:5, 6 (CSB).

Chapter Eleven

Jehovah Maccaddeshem

Each of the many names of God reveals an aspect of His character that assists us to know Him better. Life eternal, wrote John, is to know God and Jesus Christ. [199]

Ēlohim unveils for us the Creator, the Preserver, and the Keeper of His Covenants.

Yahweh proclaims the Lord as holiness, the revealer of truth, the righteous one, and our redeemer.

Ēl-Shaddai is our Almighty God, our all-sufficient supplier, the bestower of power, gifts, blessings, and the one who makes us prosperous.

---

[199] See John 17:3.

Adonai depicts the Lord as our Sovereign God, and the owner of all things.

Jehovah-*Jireh*, the Lord will provide, portrays a god who will see our needs and meet them.

Jehovah-*Nissi* represents the banner under which we are brought together and given victory over our enemies.

In this chapter we will look at *Yahweh Maccaddeshcem* (or Jehovah M'Kaddesh), the Lord who sanctifies us. [200] The word *kaddosh* means holy, to dedicate, set apart, sanctify. In the book of Exodus, the Lord tells Moses to instruct the Israelites to keep the sabbath as a sign between them and the Lord and then He adds: "that you may know that I am the Lord who sanctifies you." [201]

The first mention of God's sanctifying power comes from Genesis where God declares the seventh day as sacred:

"God blessed the seventh day and made it holy [sanctified it]: because on it he ceased all the work that he had been doing in creation." [202]

---

[200] See Lev. 20:7, 8.
[201] Exo. 31:13.
[202] Gen. 2:3.

The word "sanctify" appears 700 times in the Bible. Primarily, it means to set apart or declare holy; consecrate; make legitimate or binding by religious sanction; free from sin; purify; cause to be morally right or acceptable.

Think about the following synonyms of the word sanctify and consider how Jehovah M'Kaddesh implements each one into our relationship with Him:

Make holy · make sacred · bless · hallow · dedicate to God · anoint · ordain · approve · sanction · justify · vindicate · indorse · support · back · ratify · confirm · warrant · permit · allow · accredit · authorize · legitimize · purify · cleanse · free from sin · absolve · unburden · redeem.

Do we recognize the way the Lord, Jehovah M'Kaddesh, works in our lives to fulfill each of these needs? How lost we would be without His divine intervention!

God demands holiness. Unfortunately, we cannot be holy in and of ourselves. We cannot through our personal strength or efforts ever attain holiness on our own, so we have *Yahweh Maccaddeshcem*, "The God Who Makes Holy." We are sanctified through the blood of Jesus Christ and presented "holy, without blemish, and blameless before him." [203] What we

---

[203] See Col. 1:22.

cannot achieve, Christ is willing to accomplish for us if we will allow it.

"Now may the God of peace Himself make you completely holy [sanctify you entirely]; and may your spirit and soul and body be kept entirely blameless at the coming of our Lord Jesus Christ." [204]

When we put our trust in Christ, demonstrating faith in Him as our Savior, we can be sanctified or made holy. Paul tells us:

"And every priest stands day after day serving and offering the same sacrifices again and again—sacrifices that can never take away sins. But when this priest (Jesus Christ) had offered one sacrifice for sins for all time, he sat down at the right hand of God... for by one offering he has perfected for all time those who are made holy." [205]

In spite of the fact that every human fails to achieve perfection, the one true, living, loving God has provided a way to sanctify us. How beautiful! Christ, our Savior, atoned for our sins and sacrificed His own life so that we can be perfected and sanctified through Him. Jehovah M'Kaddesh removes all our imperfections. This does not mean that we *are* perfect; it means that each moment we mess up, a perfect God

---

[204] 1 Thes. 5:23.
[205] Heb. 10:11-14.

will not look on that imperfection but choose instead to forgive us through Christ's accomplished effort on our behalf.

"God made the one who did not know sin to be sin for us, so that in him we would become the righteousness of God." [206]

So, just how does Jehovah-M'Kaddesh bring about our sanctification?

We can be sanctified as we adhere to the truth of His word.

"Set them apart [sanctify them] in the truth: your word is truth. Just as you sent me into the world, so I sent them into the world. And I set myself apart [sanctify myself] on their behalf, so that they may be truly set apart [sanctified]." [207]

Sometimes, as is the case with all children, we require a little chastisement.

"For they disciplined us for a little while as seemed good to them, but he does so for our benefit, that we may share his holiness.

---

[206] 2 Cor. 5:21.
[207] John 17:17-19.

"Now all discipline seems painful at the time, not joyful. But later it produces the fruit of peace and righteousness for those trained by it." [208]

Perhaps the most effective way is through personal discipline.

"Therefore come out from their midst, and be separate, says the Lord, and touch no unclean thing; and I will welcome you." [209]

"Therefore I exhort you, brothers and sisters, by the mercies of God, to present your bodies a sacrifice—alive, holy, and pleasing to God—which is your reasonable service.

"Do not be conformed to this present world: but be transformed by the renewing of your mind, so that you may test and approve what is the will of God—what is good, well-pleasing and perfect." [210]

Our Father in Heaven desires to do great things in us and through us. [211] He has magnificent plans for us. [212] These plans constitute our purpose in life and are realized through His sanctification. Paul reminds us that it is God who works in us "both to will and to do for

---

[208] Heb. 12:10, 11.
[209] 2 Cor. 6:17.
[210] Rom. 12:1, 2.
[211] Eph. 2:10.
[212] Jer. 29:11.

His good pleasure." [213] He equips and empowers us for the work that we are called to, and the abundant life He has planned for us. [214]

What then, is our part in all of this?

Paul said: "I have been crucified with Christ, and it is no longer I who live, but Christ lives in me. So the life I now live in the body, I live because of the faithfulness of the Son of God, who loved me and gave himself for me." [215]

Living by faith in the Son of God—that is our part. We are told to work out our salvation with "fear and trembling," meaning that we are to take seriously the sacrifice that Christ made for us and diligently live a life of faith. That is how we fulfill the call of *Yahweh Maccaddeshcem* in our lives.

Sometimes we question why we were ever born or what our purpose is on this planet. God knows our sacred purpose. He has made us and set us apart to complete His will and to do His good pleasure. We are called to something great! We are designated and set apart for a marvelous work through God.

Fortunately, we don't need to drive ourselves crazy trying to figure out what sacred purpose we have

---

[213] Phil. 2:13 (KJV).
[214] John 10:10.
[215] Gal. 2:20.

been placed on earth for. Simply put, we are called to love Him and to love our neighbors. His further purposes will become clear to us as we obey His commandment to love. We may not feel good enough or important enough to catch the attention of the Almighty, but God will make us everything He needs and better so that we may accomplish His sacred purposes.

If we desire to see our purpose fulfilled, we simply need to begin acting in love toward God and to our neighbor. We should honor His words and commands and, as we seek Him, He will reveal Himself to us. Instead of spending all our time seeking our sacred purpose or calling, let's seek the One who called us to the purpose. It is then that we will come face to face with our sacred mission on earth.

We are so loved by God that He has offered to sanctify us, set us apart for His sacred purpose, make us holy, and remove all our imperfections. *Yahweh-Maccaddeshem,* the Lord is our sanctifier. He forgives our sins. His Spirit influences our lives to help us become like Him: pure, loving, and truthful. [216]

---

[216] Exo. 31:13; Lev. 20:8; Eze. 37:28.

Chapter Twelve

Ēl-Roi Sees Us

Have you ever wondered, out of all the billions of people on this planet, does God even know that you exist? Are you just an unknown entity in a mass of humanity or could God really single you out as an individual?

Stephen Altrogge writes: "Jesus knows us fully... He knows us better than we know ourselves. And He also knows suffering on an intense, personal level... He meets us in our downcast state and pours out grace upon us." [217]

---

[217] Altrogge, Stephen. *The Blazing Center Blog.*

God is not blind to our predicaments. Our dilemmas and difficulties have not caught Him off guard (although they may have taken us by surprise). God is omniscient, He knows all. He sees exactly what is happening to us every second of the day—good and bad. Our conditions and circumstances—our very life—is before his eyes continuously. Nothing escapes His divine notice or attention.

In today's difficult times, when we feel vulnerable, invisible, and lost, we discover hope and power in the name *Ēl-Roi*. We know God as *Ēlohim* and Yahweh, but what do we know about *Ēl-Roi*?

Ro'iy in the original Hebrew can be translated as shepherd, or as seeing, looking, or gazing. When we feel lonely and abandoned, we can be assured that God is with us. He sees and knows us. He hears the cry of our heart, and He loves us more than we could ever imagine. He will guide us and fill our heart with gladness.

Unlike many of the names for God, we only find *Ēl-Roi*, "the strong one who sees," once throughout the Scriptures, and it comes from a rather unique and unusual setting. The first person to call God by the name *Ēl-Roi* was Hagar, a maidservant to Sarai, Abram's wife. [218]

---

[218] See Gen. 16.

God promised Abram (the father and patriarch of the Jewish nation) that He would "give all the land that you see to you and your descendants forever. And I will make your descendants like the dust of the earth, so that if anyone is able to count the dust of the earth, then your descendants also can be counted." [219]

Abram shared the news of God's promises with his wife, but as the months turned into years, Sarai grew impatient. God had promised Abram offspring that would form a great nation, [220] but it became a bit problematic not having any children. Sarai told Abram that the Lord had kept her from having children and that he should sleep with her maidservant, that perhaps they could build a family through her. It was common in ancient times for an infertile wife to offer her maid to preserve the family line, so Abram agreed to Sarai's proposal and Hagar conceived a child.

And here the drama begins. When Hagar learned that she was pregnant, she began to despise her mistress. Sarai became jealous and blamed Abram for the tension that this situation had caused. Sarai basically told Abram: "This is all your fault! I put my servant into your arms, but now that she's pregnant she treats me with contempt." [221]

---

[219] Gen. 13:15, 16.
[220] See Gen. 12:2, 3.
[221] See Gen. 16:5, 6.

Sarai, in turn, treated Hagar so harshly that she finally ran away. In her despair, Hagar felt scared, lonely, and unloved. She wondered, perhaps, if anyone at all cared about her or what she and her unborn child were going through. That is when the angel of the Lord found Hagar in the desert and said to her: "Hagar, servant of Sarai, where have you come from, and where are you going?"

She replied: "I'm running away from my mistress, Sarai." But the Lord's angel said to her: "Return to your mistress, and submit to her authority." Then he added, "I will greatly multiply your descendants so that they will be too numerous to count."

And the angel also said, "You are now pregnant and are about to give birth to a son. You are to name him Ishmael (which means 'God hears'), for the Lord has heard your painful groans." [222]

Hagar, an abused slave, was astonished that God had seen her sorrow and had heard her petitions. She was astounded that God had cared for her in her difficulty and had spoken with her.

"So Hagar named the Lord who spoke to her, 'You are the God who sees me' (*Ēl-Roi*), for she said, 'Here have I seen one who sees me.'"

---

[222] Gen. 16:8-11.

Many of the names for God include *Ēl*. *Ēl* typically refers to God but *Roi* defines a distinct attribute of God's character: *Ēl-Roi* "The God who sees me." Think of the kindness and care that this name possesses as it points to God's personality. He is one who searches after us, who follows us with goodness. He is the one who sees us when we feel lonely, distraught and on our own. Whenever we need a reminder that God is close, the name *Ēl-Roi* assures us that God is watching over all. He sees the affairs of His children and knows when we feel lost and unloved.

A striking concept in Hagar's story is that every time Sarai or Abram mentioned Hagar, she is referred to simply as a slave or maidservant. [223] It must have been demoralizing for Hagar. But when God found Hagar in the desert, the first word he spoke was her name, "Hagar." [224]

When Hagar ran away from those that she felt hurt and betrayed her, God surrounded her with love and care. He didn't abandon her in her time of need, and He will not leave us alone in our difficult moments. The name *Ēl-Roi* reminds us that God is always close. He sees us even when we feel that no one else does, and He truly cares.

---

[223] See Gen.16:2, 5, 6.
[224] Gen. 16:8.

Can we relate to Hagar in any way? Perhaps not to her particular situation, but can we empathize with the emotions she experienced: fear, loneliness, feeling unloved and abandoned?

Has a spouse deserted you and your children? Have you lost your job or your home? Were you neglected or abused as a child? Does your employer overlook all the hard work that you do? Has a friend hurt or betrayed you?

So much significance is encompassed within the name Ēl-Roi. It is so descriptive of the character and nature of God. When we feel invisible and forgotten, God still sees us. He witnesses our struggles and stands beside us. The one who sees the sparrows and cares for them [225] will also see and care for us in our greatest time of need. Just as God saw Hagar, He sees us as well. Ēl-Roi is the one who numbers the hairs on our head [226] and knows everything about us. He is concerned and cares for us. Ēl-Roi knows our past, present, and He knows our future as well. When we pray to Ēl-Roi, we are praying to the one who knows everything about us.

Even the most watchful parent must sleep sometime. But the Scriptures assure us that God never

---

[225] Matt. 6:26.
[226] See Luke 12:7.

slumbers. He never looks one direction while we sneak off in another. He never misses a millisecond of what is happening in our lives or anywhere on earth.

"The eyes of the Lord search the whole earth in order to strengthen those whose hearts are fully committed to him." [227]

If we feel frail, fragile, or weak confronting the challenges we face, we can gain renewed strength by increasing our commitment to Christ. When we decide to obey fully, to follow completely, and to keep our eyes fastened on God, then Ēl-Roi will take pleasure in watching over us. Our hearts will grow stronger, and our confidence grow deeper without our even realizing how or when it happened.

During her difficulties, Hagar learned that Ēl-Roi was watching over her. God watches over us, too.

"He will not let you stumble; the one who watches over you will not slumber." [228]

We can easily recite ample instances of God seeing the unseen in society. Christ healed lepers, the blind, and those possessed by demons. He conversed with an outcast Samaritan woman at the well. We

---

[227] 2 Chron. 16:9.
[228] Psa. 121:3.

encounter countless occasions in Scripture where God chooses to see the unseen.

How about today? How does knowing God as *Ēl-Roi*, the God who sees us, impact our lives? Do we still believe we have a God who sees us—especially when we feel most invisible? In our world, it becomes easy to believe that God has forgotten us, or that He simply doesn't see us. When we open our eyes to the blessings around us, we will discover His fingerprints everywhere and in everything.

"The Lord watches over you—the Lord is your shade at your right hand; the sun will not harm you by day, nor the moon by night. The Lord will keep you from all harm—he will watch over your life; the Lord will watch over your coming and going both now and forevermore." [229]

In the middle of a crisis, amid the storm, we may feel that God has fallen asleep, and our little boat is about to capsize. [230] In that moment, we may feel as though God has abandoned us, but God sees us! We are His "workmanship, created in Christ Jesus for good works, which God prepared beforehand, that we should walk in them." [231] That is how well God knows us.

---

[229] Psa. 121:5-8.
[230] See Mark 4:35-41.
[231] Eph. 2:10.

As individuals, we are known by Him! He took an intimate interest in forming us and we are "fearfully and wonderfully made... all of His works are wonderful." [232] He loves us so much that He sent His only son, Jesus Christ, to suffer and die a horrific death, so that we could be forgiven and reconciled back to God. God wants that relationship with us. [233]

Jesus was born a king. He could have chosen to enjoy a comfortable life and to hang out with all the cool high priests, Pharisees, and Sadducees. He could have ruled the Roman Empire if He had wanted to! Instead, He devoted his time, His attention, and His care to society's lowest creatures. He advocated for tax collectors, prostitutes, and sinners.

He saw them.

When we feel like we have strayed too far from the love of God, we can remember how Christ saw everyone who had been ushered to the sidelines. He healed them. He spoke with them. He ate with them. He loved them.

When we find ourselves, as Hagar did, alone, shunned and suffering, and we question: "Does anyone care about me? Does anyone know what I'm going through? Does God even see what's happening to me

---

[232] Psa. 139:13, 14.
[233] See John 3:16; Rom. 5:8.

and how horrific it is?" The answer is: Yes, He does! Like Hagar, God sees us.

Ēl-Roi came to Hagar. He sought her out and arrived at the time of her greatest need. When no one else cared enough to show her a thread of decency, God did. It is no different for us. God knows our names. We are His and He knows each of His "sheep" by name. [234] Our names are "engraved" on the palm of His hand. [235] The implication of being engraved carries a much deeper significance than simply being written. To engrave means to cut or carve into God's palm, making it permanent and unerasable.

"The Father of compassion and the God of all comfort" [236] soothed Hagar's worries and healed her weary, wounded heart. God also promises that He will "never leave you nor forsake you." [237] It is during our times of greatest need that *Ēl-Roi* pours out His grace and mercy on us. [238]

---

[234] See John 10:3.
[235] See Isa. 49:16.
[236] Psa. 147:3.
[237] Duet. 31:6.
[238] See Heb. 4:14-16.

Chapter Thirteen

Yahweh Rohi – My Shepherd

As a young boy, my father worked herding sheep at the base of the Grand Teton Mountains. Shepherding was also a familiar and focal profession throughout Old Testament times. In those days, shepherds would traverse the countryside, residing in tents while securing pasture for their flocks. They were responsible for finding fresh pastures for the sheep in settings that provided shelter from heat, from storms and from predators.

The duty of a shepherd was to carefully plan to ensure the flock had sufficient grass and water. The necessity of preventing the sheep from straying and providing protection from thieves and wild animals required that the shepherd remain with the sheep continuously. They would spend so much time together that individual sheep, even when mixed with other flocks, could recognize the voice of their shepherd, and came immediately when called.

YHWH Rohi (pronounced Row-ee) means "the Lord my Shepherd." The Hebrew word *rohi* (or *ro'i* or *ro'eh*) is both a noun and a verb, signifying "a shepherd" or "a pasture", as well as "to shepherd" or "to pasture." The word *rohi* comes from the Hebrew word *raah* which means to feed and tend domestic animals by pasturing them. It can also be translated as feeder, keeper, pastor, herdsman, and shepherd. An extended translation of the word as a noun is "friend" or "companion."

God demonstrates, at one time or another, all these character qualities to His people. The name *Yahweh Rohi* reveals the deep spiritual, mental and emotional intimacy God desires to develop with His people. He craves a close personal connection in every aspect of our existence where we can and would depend on Him for all our needs. God yearns to be the reason we have no want.

"The Lord is my shepherd; I shall not want." [239]

YHWH Rohi is the name used for God by David. This opening assertion of Psalm 23 joins the personal name for God, *Yahweh* (Jehovah), with a descriptive name for God, *rohi* (my Shepherd). *YHWH Rohi* reveals

---

[239] Psa. 23:1.

God's caring nature as a provider of physical as well as spiritual sustenance.

David was not the first to refer to God as our Shepherd. Jacob (Israel) called God "my Shepherd" and "the shepherd, the stone of Israel." [240] Another of the Psalms also addresses God as the "Shepherd of Israel." [241] The prophet Ezekiel fused together the functions of shepherd, servant, and prince in his prophecy of the coming Messiah. [242] Elsewhere God is simply called the Shepherd.

Primarily, it is Psalm 23 that revels the love that God is willing to lavish on his sheep:

"The Lord is my shepherd..."

YHWH Rohi supplies our needs:
"I shall not want... my cup runneth over."
I have all that I need... my cup overflows.

YHWH Rohi restores our strength:
"He maketh me to lie down in green pastures... He restoreth my soul."

---

[240] Gen. 48:15.
[241] Psa. 80:1.
[242] Ezek. 34:23, 24; 37:24, 25.

He allows me to rest in green meadows... He renews my strength.

YHWH Rohi leads us:
"He leadeth me beside the still waters... he leadeth me in the paths of righteousness."
He leads me beside peaceful streams... He guides me along right paths.

YHWH Rohi makes us fearless:
"I will fear no evil."
I will not be afraid.

YHWH Rohi stands at our side:
"For thou art with me."
For you are close beside me.

YHWH Rohi reassures us:
"Thy rod and thy staff they comfort me."
Your rod and your staff protect and comfort me.

YHWH Rohi honors us:
"Thou preparest a table for me in the presence of mine enemies: thou anointest my head with oil."

You prepare a feast for me right in front of my enemies. You pour oil on my head.

YHWH Rohi pursues us:
"Goodness and mercy shall follow me all the days of my life."
Your goodness and love will follow me all the days of my life.

YHWH Rohi saves us eternally:
"I will dwell in the house of the Lord forever." [243]
I will live in the Lord's house forever.

For ancient Israel, the word "shepherd" became a metaphor for kings and was also applied to religious leaders. Israel's leaders, however, were often reprimanded for their failure to properly watch over the flock of God. God issued a severe warning to false shepherds who had authority to lead but who gave up that responsibility to better serve themselves. They were most likely good people who eventually became greedy and self-serving.

While our Shepherd does so much for us, we, as sheep, have a responsibility to not be lead astray. We must understand that more than one shepherd calls to

---

[243] See Ps. 23.

us. Ezekiel 34 exposes how false shepherds care only for themselves. We should recognize and run from them and seek out the one true Shepherd.

"Shepherds of Israel who have been feeding yourselves! Should not shepherds feed the sheep?"

The false shepherds feed themselves and not their flock.

"You eat the fat, you clothe yourselves with the wool, you slaughter the fat ones, but you do not feed the sheep."

The false shepherds do for themselves, taking the finest things life has to offer.

"The weak you have not strengthened, the sick you have not healed, the injured you have not bound up, the strayed you have not brought back, the lost you have not sought, and with force and harshness you have ruled them." [244]

False shepherds do not strengthen the weak. They do not heal the sick or bandage the injured. False shepherds do not bring back the strays or seek after the lost. False shepherds rule with force and harshness.

Do we recognize *Yahweh Roi* as our shepherd? Do we listen to hear His voice calling us or do we seek

---

[244] See Ezek. 34:2-4.

the enticements of a false shepherd? Can we even distinguish the voice of the one true Shepherd? When we decide to submit our will to God's, when we pray and listen for His quiet whisperings within our hearts, we will then begin to recognize His voice calling us to safety.

Matthew recites a prophecy of Micah regarding Bethlehem: "Out of you will come a ruler who will shepherd my people Israel." [245] Jesus was born in Bethlehem, of the line of David, the ultimate shepherd-ruler. *Rohi,* or the Greek equivalent (*poiman `o kalos*) is a name Jesus used to refer to himself as a claim to deity and to his status as the God of David:

"I am the good shepherd. The good shepherd lays down his life for the sheep..." [246]

The New Testament ascribes several shepherd names to Jesus: Good Shepherd, Great Shepherd of the sheep, Shepherd and guardian of our souls, and Chief Shepherd. Jesus cares for us in the same way a shepherd tends to his sheep. He provides for us refreshing water and lush, green pastures. He restores our strength.

Do you feel safe and cared for?

The comforting name of *Yahweh Roi* is an assurance that the Good Shepherd, the promised

---

[245] Matt. 2:6; See also Mic. 5:2.
[246] John 10:11.

Messiah Jesus Christ, would offer His life for His sheep and offer redemption through His blood so that we could obtain salvation, peace, eternal life, and a restored relationship with God.

When we recognize God as *Yahweh-Rohi*, our shepherd,[247] we can expect that He will protect us and keep us safe through troubling times. This may not mean that we will forego experiencing the hurtful, the bad, the sorrowful side of life, but the good Shepherd will lead us through it. We will have the strength to withstand any trial because He will always be at our side.

God is our shepherd. He knows the green pastures and how to steer us along dangerous paths until we reach the pleasant meadows. He knows all our needs. Whether our rough terrain be physical or spiritual, emotional or mental, we can trust the Lord to lead us and guide us. He knows what is ahead.

Listen carefully and follow His voice as the good Shepherd navigates you through the bumpy, uneven landscape of life.

---

[247] Psalms 23, 80:1, 95:7; Isa. 40:11, Jer. 31:10; Eze. 34:12,23.

Chapter Fourteen

Erkamka – I Love You

In Chapter 6 we discussed the divine name *Ēl-Shaddai*, the name that inspired the beautiful song written by Michael Card and popularized by Amy Grant. The song praises God with these beautiful words:

> "El Shaddai, El Shaddai, El Elyon na Adonai
> Age to age You're still the same
> By the power of Your name.
> El Shaddai, El Shaddai, Erkamka na Adonai
> We will praise and lift You high
> El Shaddai."

Although we love this song, few of us are familiar with the meaning of *Erkamka na Adonai*. In fact, when I googled *Erkamka*, the definitions I uncovered were:

"This is a butchery of the Hebrew language" and "This is a mixture of Hebrew and gibberish. It means nothing at all."

Due to poor transliteration, *Erkamka* is basically nonsensical in Hebrew. It should be: *Erachamcha*. However, the Hebrew text found in Psalm 18:1 can uncover the meaning of *Erkamka na Adonai* for us.

ב וַיֹּאמַר-- אֶרְחָמְךָ יְהוָה חִזְקִי

"And he said: I love thee, O LORD, my strength." [248]

When asked for the meaning of the words "Erkamka na Adonai," Michael Card wrote that the expression means "We will love You, Oh, Lord." [249]

The word *Adonai* is a title applied to God. The word is translated "Lord" or "My Lord." A detailed description of Adonai is given in Chapter 7 of this book.

The Hebrew word *nā* is a particle of entreaty or exhortation. When the word is used in the text, it carries the idea of "please," "I pray," or "now." Strong's Concordance offers this definition:

"A primitive particle of incitement and entreaty, which may usually be rendered: 'I pray,' 'now,' or 'then;'

---

[248] Psa. 18:1.
[249] Card, Michael, *Immanuel: Reflections on the Life of Christ.* Nashville, TN: Thomas Nelson, Inc., 1990. Pp. 200, 201.

added mostly to verbs (in the Imperative or Future), or to interjections, occasionally to an adverb or conjunction -- I beseech (pray) thee (you), go to, now, oh." [250]

Psalm 118, one of the psalmist's prayers to the Lord, is an example the use of *nā*:

"We beseech Thee, O LORD, save now." [251]

The expression "save now" in Hebrew is *hôshî'ânā*, the very same proclamation spoken by the people of Jerusalem when they welcomed Jesus with shouts of "Hosanna." [252] The particle *nā* is not in the Hebrew text of Psalm 18:1. It is possible that it was written into the song to represent the "O" in "O LORD."

Erkamka comes from the beginning of Psalm 18:1. The transliteration of these Hebrew words into English reads as follows:

'erḥāmekā yhwh ḥizqî

"I love you, O LORD, my strength" [253]

The Hebrew word for love is רחם (*rāḥam*), a word that means "to have mercy," "to be compassionate."

---

[250] Strong's Exhaustive Concordance online.
[251] Psa. 118:25 (JPS).
[252] Mark 11:9. Note: The Complete Jewish Bible translates this as: "Please! Deliver us."
[253] Psa. 18:1 (ESV).

Psalm 18:1 is the only place where the Hebrew Bible uses 'erḥāmekā as love and where *Yahweh* appears as the object of the verb *rāḥam*. (This is normally an Aramaic usage.) Hebrew uses 'erḥāmekā in the context of compassion rather than love. The Strong Concordance transliterates the word *rāḥam* as *rakham*. *'Erḥāmekā* would then naturally be translated as "erkamka," dropping the "h" of *rakham* and eliminating the second "e."

The verb *'erḥāmekā* is first person, making the proper translation out to be "I love you," not "we will love you." The English Standard Version of the Bible translates Psalm 18:1 as: "I love you, O LORD." The Complete Jewish Bible translates the verse as: "I love you, ADONAI."

Chapter Fifteen

Yahweh Rapha – Our Healer

Freed from 400 years of captivity in Egypt, the Israelites ventured toward the Promised Land, only to find themselves, as Tony Evans puts it, caught "between a rock and a wet place"—the Red Sea. [254] They complained and God delivered them by dividing the water, allowing them to cross the sea on dry land. The waters returned and drowned the pursuing Egyptian army and the Israelites rejoiced with a song of praise and triumph to the Lord:

---

[254] Evans, Tony, *The Power of God's Names,* Harvest House Publishers, Kindle Edition, p. 154.

"The Lord is my strength and my song; he has become my salvation. He is my God and I will praise him, my father's God, and I will exalt him.

"Who among the gods is like you, O Lord? Who is like you—majestic in holiness, awesome in glory, working wonders?

"In your unfailing love you will lead the people you have redeemed. In your strength you will guide them to your holy dwelling." [255]

Nothing can compare to God's unfailing love and mighty strength for His people, and for a moment, the children of Israel were thankful for God's remarkable power, goodness and salvation, and their hearts surged with praise. But that would all change.

Moses led them deeper into the Desert of Shur where "for three days they traveled... without finding water." [256] No potable water, anyway. Eventually, they came to a body of water, but, to their dismay, they could not drink it.

"When they came to Marah, they could not drink the waters of Marah, for they were bitter." [257]

---

[255] Exo. 15:2, 11, 13 (NIV).
[256] Exo. 15:22.
[257] Exo. 15:23.

Of course, the Israelites grouched and griped. The water wasn't the only bitterness in that desert; the souls of the Israelites turned bitter as well. They had already forgotten how grateful they had been for God's deliverance. They "grumbled against Moses, saying, 'What are we to drink?'" [258] Apparently, they had also forgotten that God's great power over the waters. Moses prayed to the Lord, and "the Lord showed him a piece of wood." [259] Following God's directive, Moses threw the wood into the waters of Marah and, miraculously, "the water became fit to drink." [260]

In just seventy-two hours, the children of Israel failed to remember the goodness of God and their miraculous deliverance out of Egypt. They grumbled against Moses and unbelief dominated their minds. Even after they witnessed countless miraculous acts of God's power in liberating them from Egypt, they did not believe that God Almighty could provide water for them to drink. But once again, God came to their rescue.

Immediately after the Lord "healed" the waters of Marah, He identified Himself to the Israelites as *Yahweh-Rapha*: "I am the Lord, who heals you." [261] The Israelites were not sick. They were just extremely

---

[258] Exo. 15:24.
[259] Ibid. 25.
[260] Ibid. 25.
[261] Ibid. 26.

thirsty. So why did God reveal Himself to them as *Yahweh Rapha*—the God who heals?

It is amazing that God lovingly chose this moment to reveal to the Israelites this important characteristic of His nature and His covenant promise of healing. The Israelites had suffered terribly while in Egypt and were delighted to have their freedom, but life was still difficult for them. They had to rely on God for everything. When conditions and circumstances became difficult, their hearts filled with resentment. God knew their greatest need was not water. What they really needed was healing from bitterness and pain.

That is the context in which God shows Himself as "the LORD who heals."

Israel had begun to be corrupted from within by a spirit and attitude of bitterness that stemmed from their captivity in Egypt. When God doesn't work in our life in the way we think He should, do we also grow bitter? I relate a little too much with the Israelites in this sense. In my difficulties, I forget that God has great plans for me. I need to remember not to complain. Can you relate as well?

The Lord longs to heal us from resentfulness, bitterness, and pride if we will just trust and obey Him. Israel's bitterness was hindering them from trusting God and diligently following His will. This bitterness could be infectious, corrupting them physically, mentally, emotionally, and spiritually. *Yahweh-Rapha* was tenderly showing His people that He is the healer of all bitterness in the human heart and soul.

Working through Moses and a piece of wood, God reminded the Israelites of the diseases and plagues that afflicted the Egyptians—plagues of boils, the death of livestock, devastating hail, etc.—due to their oppression of the Hebrew slaves. God made it evident to the Israelites that they must obey Him so that they would not suffer similar afflictions. Then He gives the Israelites a promise:

"I will not bring on you any of the diseases I brought on the Egyptians." [262]

The promise was conditional; the Israelites were required to "diligently listen to the voice of the Lord your God, and do that which is right in his eyes, and give ear to his commandments and keep all his statutes." [263]

God is our Healer in both body and spirit. When we follow God's directions, things go well for us. He desires we obey His commands, so that we may be blessed. If the space in our lives is filled with sin, then there is no room for God to bless us.

---

[262] Ibid. 26.
[263] Exo. 15:26, (ESV; cf. Deuteronomy 30).

Bitterness impedes the healing power of the Lord and obstructs the heart from loving and serving Him. It opens the floodgates to disease in the body, the emotions, the mind, and the soul. *Yahweh-Rapha* can completely remove the stinging numbness and deep pain of bitterness and restore sweet joy and peace to every fiber of our being. God wants our souls to bathe in the sweetness of His love, where bitterness has no place. His healing balm can remove all the bitterness.

Bitterness is often the root of other illnesses that inflict and infect us. A bitter soul or a sour mind can wreak havoc on the physical body. The mind, body and spirit cannot flourish when a heart is contaminated with bitterness. *Yahweh-Rapha* can make all the bitter areas of our life sweet again.

God doesn't just heal water; He heals people. The healing of the waters was merely a demonstration of God's power to overcome any impurity, contamination, or corruption. This power was at work on the Israelites as the Lord brought them into the Promised Land.

The name *Yahweh-Rapha* brings hope to the many who have prayed for healing and deliverance from debilitating diseases, agonizing illnesses, and excruciating circumstances. God understands we need His healing, and He promises to redeem every hurt in our lives. *Yahweh-Rapha* brings health in every category of life.

Healing is not simply a part of God's name; it is a vital characteristic of His nature. *Yahweh-Rapha* is the only true source of all healing and restoration. We know that God is love; we also should recognize that God is healing. Healing is not a part-time thing or a side job that God dapples in occasionally when the mood strikes Him; healing is what God is.

Yahweh-Rapha has the power to heal physically,[264] emotionally,[265] mentally,[266] and spiritually.[267] God not only heals the body, but He heals the soul, the mind, and the emotions. *Yahweh-Rapha* is the cure for every single sickness, disease, and infirmity that has ever inflicted the body and mind of humanity. Neither impurity of body nor impurity of soul can withstand the purifying, healing power of *Yahweh-Rapha*.

Our healing may not always come in the moment or in the manner we would choose, and that can be difficult to accept and endure. But *Yahweh-Rapha* offers this hope and assurance: we will live eternally, free from the burdens we've carried here in

---

[264] 2 Kings 5:10.
[265] Ps. 34:18.
[266] Dan. 4:34.
[267] Ps. 103:2, 3.

this life. Jesus promises to make all things new, and God will wipe away every tear.

Sometimes, I believe, God utilizes our illnesses to get our attention. A Grecian doctor hypothesized that when we are in good health, our focus is fixed on what is around us on a horizontal level. When we are sick, on the other hand, bed-ridden and lying on our backs, our observation is upward or heavenward, and we are more open to seeing what God wants us to change in our lives and in our natures.

Yahweh-Rapha longs to tenderly cure and cleanse us to a complete condition of health and renewal. Those who think they are spiritually whole, however, will never seek a cure for their sinful nature. As Jesus explained: "It is not the healthy who need a doctor, but the sick. I have not come to call the righteous, but sinners." [268]

Yahweh-Rapha is not a God of sickness but of health; not of disease but of wholeness; not of destruction but of restoration. He mends and makes whole; He doesn't tear apart. He is a God of life not of death. *Yahweh-Rapha* is the God of all health and healing.

---

[268] Mark 2:17.

The Great Physician

A loving Father reached out to a world broken with sickness and heartache and sent His only begotten Son, Jesus Christ, the Great Physician, the remarkable healer of the diseased, the sick, and the brokenhearted. The Gospels powerfully characterize Christ carrying out His Father's will by healing every infirmity of mind and body among His people.

Jesus Christ proved Himself to be the Great Physician who healed the sick. In Galilee, from town to town, He healed "every disease and sickness among the people." [269] In Judea "large crowds followed him, and he healed them there." [270] In fact, "wherever he went—into villages, towns or countryside—they placed the sick in the marketplaces. They begged him to let them touch even the edge of his cloak, and all who touched it were healed." [271] Jesus healed people physically and He also healed them spiritually by forgiving their sins. [272]

"Because of his wounds," declares Isaiah, "we are healed." [273] Jesus Christ suffered death to give us life. He paid the price for our sins. He was the promised

---

[269] Matt. 4:23.
[270] Matt. 19:2.
[271] Mark 6:56.
[272] Luke 5:20.
[273] Isa: 1:7.

healer from the Old Testament who reveals to us the healing heart of God. [274]

Not every illness is a result of our personal sins, but every disease is ultimately the result of sin. Sickness and disease did not originate with God but entered the world through the fall of Adam and the corruption of sin that infiltrated our world. We became tarnished by sin, sorrow, evil and the innumerable ailments that plague our physical, emotional, mental, and spiritual beings. When Adam and Eve disobeyed God in the garden, the whole world was brought under the bondage of decay.

"For the creation was subjected to frustration, not by its own choice, but by the will of the one who subjected it, in hope that the creation itself will be liberated from its bondage to decay and brought into the freedom and glory of the children of God." [275]

All humanity grieves and groans under the grueling burden of the Fall. Its affliction brought on disease, death, and depression; famine, fear, and futility; hurt, heartache, and hopelessness; loneliness, longing, and loss. In short, everything that is contrary to God's design and desire for His creation. That decay is

---

[274] Exo. 15:26; 2 Chron. 7:14; Psa. 6:2, 41:4, 103:3, 147:3; Isa. 19:22, 30:36, 57:18,18; Jer. 3:22, 17:14, 30:17.
[275] Rom. 8:20, 21.

behind many of the diseases that ravage our world today. We are desperately in need of a healer!

Yahweh-Rapha longs to erase these blemishes from His beautiful creation; to heal humanity, the crowning glory of His works, restoring our dignity by delivering us from the bondage of sin. Sin's decay will not be finally eradicated until Jesus comes again. But we know that it will be eradicated, because when Christ returns, He will restore the earth to its original condition. This complete redemptive healing can only be accomplished through Jesus Christ.

The Broken Hearted

The human heart is fragile. Sometimes the greatest need of healing for someone is the healing of a broken and shattered heart. The heart gets broken in pieces and becomes susceptible to the ravages of sickness and disease. The heart becomes crushed, shattered, and broken by the vicious circumstances of life, and the world offers no hope of comfort or consolation.

Yahweh-Rapha promises deliverance and healing from every heartache; He will mend our broken dreams, cleanse and bandage every wound of the heart.

"The Lord is close to the brokenhearted and saves those who are crushed in spirit." [276]

All depression and despair, all misery and melancholy, all sorrow and sadness, all hopelessness and unhappiness and any other emotional or mental infirmity dissipates like morning dew in the embrace of our loving Heavenly Father, the healer of all heartache.

We may feel bitter and disappointed with family, friends, or others who have forsaken us. As children, we may have felt no one cared about us, that we'd been cast aside, worthless, and unwanted. Perhaps people inflicted our hearts with deep wounds of dishonesty and betrayal that left long scars of bitterness and unforgiveness. We may suffer from the traumatization of abuse or addiction. We may believe that we are useless, unwanted, worthless, and without hope. But that is not how the Lord sees us.

Yahweh-Rapha invites us back into His loving embrace to enjoy the full comfort of His healing presence. *Yahweh-Rapha* wants to restore us to a sound mind with a clear conscience; He wants to restore our emotional health and give us His divine peace and favor. All the bitterness that infiltrated the

---

[276] Ps. 34:18 (NIV).

world from the Fall was nailed to the cross with Christ as He defeated the power of sin, sickness, disease, and death.

The Spiritually Scarred

Yahweh Rapha heals not only emotionally, but also spiritually. This spiritual healing also involves a particular piece of wood. Just as Moses cast the wood in the waters of Marah making the bitter water sweet, Jesus Christ was crucified on a wooden cross to remove the bitter waters of sin and restore the sweet living waters of healing to all those who come to Him.

"He was pierced for our transgressions, he was crushed for our iniquities; the punishment that brought us peace was on him, and by his wounds we are healed." [277]

The wood cast into the waters at Marah is a symbol of the cross of Jesus Christ and a representation of God's ultimate healing power. The healing wood of Calvary provides redemptive healing and wholeness.

"He himself bore our sins in his body on the cross, so that we might die to sins and live for

---

[277] Isa. 53:5.

righteousness; 'by his wounds you have been healed.' For 'you were like sheep going astray,' but now you have returned to the Shepherd and Overseer of our souls." [278]

Jesus Christ broke the power of the curse and made life sweet again. God gave us a new nature and made us a new creation in Christ. The old ways of sin, sickness, pain, disease, and physical or mental infirmity have no more authority over us.

Christ's awesome redemptive work enables us to live in righteousness and reign as kings in life, enjoying the more than abundant and good life that God has so richly and freely given us in Christ. We were justified, made righteous, sanctified, made whole, given a new nature, healed, delivered, set free and glorified by our Lord's wonderful Atonement and redemption.

It is marvelous to know the Lord as *Yahweh-Rapha.* The voice of God is a voice of healing. He heals, restores, cures, and repairs everything that is broken in our lives. No matter what the disease, no matter what the infirmity, and no matter what the sickness, *Yahweh-Rapha* intensely desires to heal us.

---

[278] 2 Pet. 2:24, 25.

Healing is not just an ancient art of the past and God is not "the God formerly known as *Yahweh-Rapha.*" He does not change. He always was and always will be the covenant Lord who heals. His healing power allows us to live full and complete lives in physical, mental, emotional, and spiritual harmony. There is no physical sickness, mental infirmity, spiritual malady or disease of body and soul beyond the reach of the healing power of *Yahweh-Rapha*.

"Heal me, O Yahweh, and I shall be healed; save me, and I shall be saved: for thou art my praise." [279]

We can call upon *Yahweh-Rapha* today to heal us of our physical illnesses and to provide redemption for our sins. Through the power of the blood of the Great Physician—Jesus, we can rise from our old sinful life as new creations in eternal fellowship with God. Just as the Israelites were cleansed of their bitter hearts and resentment at the river Marah, so we can ask God to examine our hearts and cleanse them of all bitterness and pride.

---

[279] Jer. 17:14 (ASV).

Chapter Sixteen

Abba: More than 'Daddy'

Most of us have heard God referred to as "Abba, Father." The title of "Abba, Father" is only found referenced in the Bible three times in the New Testament as spoken by Jesus and the apostle Paul. So why would a title mentioned so sparingly in the Scriptures be so monumental in describing not only Jesus' and Paul's relationships with God but our relationship with Him as well?

This name of God is rich with meaning and implications for our lives. Abba is an impressively intimate form of God's name, showing us His character as our loving Father. He is the one we can fully trust, the one we can depend on, the one who cares about all our troubles and concerns. Just as an earthly father's existence in our lives should be to provide protection, security, and unconditional love, the constant presence of our heavenly Father can give us the strength and safety we need for our life's journey.

All of God's distinctive names in Scripture describe His character and are significant in different respects. However, the name "Abba, Father" is one of the most noteworthy names of God in depicting His relationship with us. Abba is an Aramaic (or, at least, Semitic) word for "Father." Abba is not a translation, but a transliteration. No word in English exists that it could be translated into. *Father* is a direct translation. *Abba* refers mainly to the spiritual relationship with God.

Considerable debate surrounds the connotation of the word Abba. Some translate it as "Daddy," symbolizing a child's characterization for his or her father. It is a common term that expresses affection, confidence, and trust. As such, it conveys God's relationship and regard for each of us as His children. He grants us the honor of being called His sons and daughters. He provides us a way to call on Him with the certain assurance that He hears us and will answer our need. In difficult and painful times, the term Abba provides the familiar sensation of being able to climb into the lap of a loving heavenly Father, and know that He is there for us, and that His arms will shelter and embrace us always. Abba implies a close, intimate relationship between a father and his child, and the simple trust a young person places in "daddy."

Some scholars believe that Abba is not a babyish expression, but a term of respect. It is Father as used by an adult child, familial, but still demonstrating reverence and respect. The definite article often used along with Abba gives the term a sense of "the Father" or "my Father." The term carries with it a sense of closeness. God is our Father. We are adopted into His family. We are made His children.

Dictionary.com defines "Abba" as the term for father in the Aramaic language, spoken by Jesus and Paul as an intimate term to characterize their personal relationships with God. It is also a term of reverence. Scripturally, the meaning of Abba includes authority and discipline along with compassion, care, protection, and provision.

In the Gospel of Mark, Jesus addresses God as "Abba, Father" in His prayer in Gethsemane.

"And He [Jesus] said, 'Abba, Father, all things are possible for You. Take this cup away from Me; nevertheless, not what I will, but what You will.'" [280]

Addressing God as "Abba, Father" in the garden of Gethsemane acknowledges the power and

---

[280] Mark 14:36.

greatness of God and the glory that will come to Him through Jesus' sacrifice. In humble admiration for His Father, Jesus makes an intimate request for God's will to be shown in the cup of Christ's suffering and sacrifice.

In Romans, "Abba, Father" is spoken in relation to the Spirit's work of adoption that makes us heirs with Christ.

"For all who are led by the Spirit of God are sons of God. For you did not receive the spirit of slavery to fall back into fear, but you have received the Spirit of adoption as sons, by whom we cry, 'Abba! Father!'

"The Spirit himself bears witness with our spirit that we are children of God, and if children, then heirs—heirs of God and fellow heirs with Christ, provided we suffer with him in order that we may also be glorified with him." [281]

We have been fully accepted as true sons and daughters into the family of God. We are heirs with Christ. We are not only witnesses and servants, but we are also part of His family and granted the right to participate in the fullness of God's plan.

In Galatians, again in the context of adoption, the Spirit within us cries out, "Abba, Father."

---

[281] Rom. 8:15.

"And because you are sons, God has sent forth the Spirit of His Son into your hearts, crying out, 'Abba, Father!'" [282]

These are the only texts containing the two words together, "Abba, Father," though they were commonly linked by early Christians. The passage from Mark is stated by Jesus, while the verses from Romans and Galatians are shared by Paul. Together, the terms Abba and Father doubly emphasize the fatherhood of God. In two different languages, we are assured of God's care for His children.

The capital 'F' used for 'Father' and the capital 'A' used for 'Abba' indicate a title rather than just a term or expression. The masculine noun 'Father' comes from the Greek, *pater* and has both literal and metaphorical meanings.

Father: Capitalization of this word denotes reference toward God. As the Father, He is acknowledged to be our creator, sustainer, and protector.

Abba: The word was originally used in prayer to God, and as such constitutes a more formal word. It is used in the New Testament attached to the Greek word *Pater*. Abba is the Aramaic equivalent of the Hebrew

---

[282] Gal. 4:6.

'father'. It gradually came to be considered a sacred proper name.

Abba is, essentially, more of a personal name. Father refers to a role or relationship. The word Abba implies total trust. The term Father addresses a specific, certain association. Used together, "Abba, Father," denotes trust and love, as well as an intimate, personal relationship.

Interestingly, in Scripture only Jesus Christ and the apostle Paul refer to God as "Abba, Father." Jesus is the Son of God and savior for all mankind; Paul was a Jew intent on destroying the concept of Christianity surrounding Jesus. Initially, these two men couldn't have been more different in the eyes of the world, yet in the eyes of God they were eternal spiritual brothers. Both Jesus and Paul demonstrated a deep connection with God, willingly submitting to a devotion that placed them in danger and facing that danger with the assurance that faith conquers all.

Abba is an Aramaic word that some people believe means "Daddy," and is a term of intimate connection between father and child, but "Daddy" is an inadequate translation. It disregards a vital aspect of Abba, and that one missing characteristic makes a world of difference.

Abba is personal, which is part of the meaning, but Daddy or Dad is an incomplete rendering. Abba is more like the English "Sir" than "Daddy." There are two elements involved in the term Abba. The two elements are: Intimacy and Obedience.

It's the obedience part that we miss when equating it to just "Daddy." Abba is not merely about intimacy; it's also about authority. It's both intimacy and obedience, so neither "Sir" nor "Daddy" are adequate translations.

One perspective we are given shows Abba as a term of endearment, intimacy, and close relationship. The other viewpoint is the concept and condition of obedience.

The true meaning of Abba is "Father, I will obey you." Both elements must be present. Each of its three uses in the New Testament—Mark 14:36, Romans 8:15, and Galatians 4:6—reveal this connotation.

Jesus addresses God as "Abba, Father." He uses Abba in his prayer in Gethsemane along with the word *Pater*, the Greek word for father, inferring a distinction with Abba that the Greek *Pater* does not convey. Abba is a word of feeling spoken from the heart, but also a word of discipleship. Both elements are captured in Mark's account of Jesus' passionate plea to God.

"Going a little farther, he fell to the ground and prayed that if possible the hour might pass from him. 'Abba, Father,' he said, 'everything is possible for you. Take this cup from me. Yet not what I will, but what you will.'" [283]

Jesus is entering His most difficult time in the Garden of Gethsemane and withdraws to be alone in an intimate prayer session with His Father. The substance of Jesus' plea expresses His willingness to obey. Jesus was connecting intimately with the Father but also expressing His submission to God. "Not what I will, but what you will." And so, He begins His prayer with the term, "Abba."

Paul demonstrates a similar connotation.

"For you did not receive a spirit that makes you a slave again to fear, but you received the Spirit of sonship. And by him we cry, 'Abba, Father.'" [284]

Paul also uses the Aramaic term Abba followed by the Greek term *Pater*. His purpose, like Jesus' is to express both intimacy and obedience. The "Spirit of sonship" in opposition to "fear" is the motivation behind his prayer. In this passage, Paul establishes the intimate relationship we have with God, as close as a father to his child. Yet, it isn't solely about intimacy. It

---

[283] Mark 14:35, 36 (NIV).
[284] Rom. 8:15.

also addresses the obedient heart of the one who cries Abba. In the preceding passages Paul reveals that the cry of "Abba, Father" is an act of submission:

"Therefore, brothers, we have an obligation—but it is not to the sinful nature, to live according to it. For if you live according to the sinful nature, you will die; but if by the Spirit you put to death the misdeeds of the body, you will live, because those who are led by the Spirit of God are sons of God. For you did not receive a spirit that makes you a slave again to fear, but you received the Spirit of sonship. And by him we cry, 'Abba, Father.'" [285]

The imperative to "put to death the misdeeds of the body" is deeply embedded within Paul's message of intimacy as being children of God. As with Jesus in Gethsemane and Romans 8, the perspective of Abba in Galatians 4 is about obedience in suffering.

Paul writes: "Because you are sons, God sent the Spirit of his Son into our hearts, the Spirit who calls out, 'Abba, Father.'" [286]

We are again, as in Romans, referred to as children of God, but here the context implies a contrast

---

[285] Ibid. 12, 13.
[286] Gal. 4:6.

between obedient slaves and obedient sons. [287] And in this verse, our obedience comes into question:

"But now that you know God—or rather are known by God—how is it that you are turning back to those weak and miserable principles? Do you wish to be enslaved by them all over again?" [288]

Yes, we are heirs, but we are heirs with a responsibility of obedience toward God and not to the rules of man.

These three New Testament passages all relate to Isaac in the Old Testament and his obedient relationship with his father Abraham. Isaac faced impending suffering and sacrificial death analogous with Jesus. Isaac was a child of promise comparable to Christ.

He carries the bundle of wood, the flint, and the knife up Mt. Moriah with his father, Abraham. Isaac is a Hebrew prior to the Jewish exile, and his story comes to us in Hebrew. He doesn't speak Aramaic but when he says "Father," he elicits the meaning of Abba, which is "Father, I will obey."

From the land of the Philistines to Mt. Moriah—a three-day journey—nothing is mentioned of Isaac questioning his father's purpose or motives until he

---

[287] See Gal. 4:1-11.
[288] Ibid. 9.

says, "Father!" [289] Isaac had travelled alongside his father and, as far as we know, he never questioned his father's intent. Surely, he must have wondered: Here is the wood and the fire, but where is the lamb for a burnt offering? Abraham's vague response that God would provide an offering allowed Isaac to continue in good faith. With the servants remaining at the bottom of the mountain, the intimacy of father and son is paired with the son's obedience to his father.

The attitude of Isaac's heart was obedience. According to the book of Jasher, Isaac, like Christ, was a willing sacrifice.

"Isaac said unto his father, I will do all that the Lord spoke to thee with joy and cheerfulness of heart.

"And Abraham again said unto Isaac his son, Is there in thy heart any thought or counsel concerning this, which is not proper? tell me my son, I pray thee, O my son conceal it not from me.

"And Isaac answered his father Abraham and said unto him, O my father, as the Lord liveth and as thy soul liveth, there is nothing in my heart to cause me to deviate either to the right or to the left from the word that he has spoken to thee.

---

[289] Gen. 22:7.

"But I am of joyful and cheerful heart in this matter, and I say, Blessed is the Lord who has this day chosen me to be a burnt offering before Him...

"And Abraham took the wood and placed it in order upon the altar which he had built.

"And he took his son Isaac and bound him in order to place him upon the wood which was upon the altar, to slay him for a burnt offering before the Lord.

"And Isaac said to his father, Bind me securely and then place me upon the altar lest I should turn and move, and break loose from the force of the knife upon my flesh and thereof profane the burnt offering." [290]

When Abraham told Isaac, "The Lord has made choice of thee my son, to be a perfect burnt offering instead of the lamb," [291] Isaac did not question, he did not refuse, and he did not run down the mountainside in fear for his life. Instead, he tells his father, "Tie me tight so the knife won't slip."

Isaac willingly submits to his father's plan to take Isaac's life as a sacrifice to God. Abraham demonstrated absolute obedience to God and Isaac demonstrated unwavering obedience to his father.

---

[290] Jasher 23:52-56, 59-61.
[291] Jasher 23:51.

Isaac's cry of "Father" on Mt. Moriah is the same cry that Jesus made—also from Mt. Moriah. [292] Both Jesus and Isaac were examining, in their own way, the plan of their father. And both, because of the intimate, trusting relationship they had with their father, were also willing to obey.

Intimacy matched with obedience is the true nature of the term Abba. It is a far richer meaning than merely "Daddy."

Even though we do not use the Aramaic word "Abba" in prayer, we must still learn to pray to our Father with a meaning resembling Abba because unless we are willing to obey, our affections of intimate sonship or daughterhood will dissipate and dry up. Our loving Father desires more than our affection; he craves our obedience.

Each one of us was created in God's image. Knowing that we are made in the same image as God establishes an unbreakable bond we share with the Father and a solid form of intimacy that cannot be replicated. God made and molded us as an earthly father does, but in a way that is closer and more personal than an earthly father ever could. He knows us more than we know ourselves and handcrafted our personalities before we were born. The term "Abba,

---

[292] See 2 Chron. 3:1.

Father" is not just an exclamation of praise or recognition. As conveyed through Jesus, Paul, and Isaac, it embodies a recognition that God knows us better than we know ourselves and that He established our paths before we took our first human steps.

When we read "Abba, Father" in the Scriptures or hear it referenced in a sermon, we should envision a Father who knows our greatest strengths, our greatest weaknesses, our very beginnings and our ultimate end. Then, yielding to His great will, we can meet Him with an intimacy that can only be felt between the Creator and the created.

God, who created and sustains all things, who is all-powerful, all-knowing, and ever-present, not only allows us but encourages us to call Him "Father." What a privilege it is! We are not guests, but family. God not only forgives us but He reveals His plan to us, as much as we are able to handle it, just as a father reveals truths to a growing child.

It is life-changing to understand what it means to be able to call the one true God our "Father" and what it means to be joint-heirs with Christ. Because of our relationship with our Abba, Father, we can approach Him with "boldness" [293] and in "full

---

[293] Heb. 10:19.

assurance of faith." [294] The Holy Spirit "testifies with our spirit that we are God's children. Now if we are children, then we are heirs—heirs of God and co-heirs with Christ." [295]

Earthly fathers fail their children. Even those who are good by human standards are not perfect. Sadly, there are many fathers who are abusive and neglectful. These men are not a reflection of God as our Father. God is the perfect Father. He does not disappoint like earthly fathers do. He does not abuse or shame. He disciplines in tenderness. [296] He is perfectly loving and intimately personal. He knows our needs, and He supplies them. [297]

God cares for us as a good father. Our salvation is secure in Him. Our earthly life is secure in Him. We can approach Him as we would a gentle father, with familial closeness interspersed with genuine respect.

---

[294] Ibid. 22.
[295] Rom. 8:16, 17.
[296] Heb. 12:7-11.
[297] Matt. 6:31-33.

Chapter Seventeen

Yahweh Shalom is Peace

Peace is more elusive than a butterfly. In my lifetime alone there have been approximately 462 wars held somewhere in the world. Relatively few of them have affected my personal feelings of peace. But other pressures, problems, changes, and challenges can certainly give us knotted muscles, sleepless nights, and restless hearts, robbing us of the peace we so desperately desire.

Still, God promises us a peace "which is far more wonderful than the human mind can understand." [298] In a world of wars, in a time of animosity, how do we experience His promise?

---

[298] Phil. 4:7.

One of God's titles in the Bible is *Yahweh-Shalom*, which means the Lord is Peace. The Hebrew word for peace, *shalom*, means wholeness in all of life, completeness, welfare, safety. The American theologian, Cornelius Plantinga, explains: "Shalom means universal flourishing, wholeness and delight—a rich state of affairs in which natural needs are satisfied and natural gifts fruitfully employed, a state of affairs that inspires joyful wonder as its Creator and Savior opens doors and welcomes the creatures in whom He delights." [299]

Throughout Scripture, the names of God reveal significant attributes about His correct character and nature. This is especially true of the name *Yahweh-Shalom* (Pronounced: yah-WEH sha-LOME). We usually find both words written separately, but seldom used together. *Yahweh-Shalom* is one of three phrases for God that was given to an altar.

The Lord is peace in Hebrew:
Yahweh shalom [300]

The Lord of peace in Greek:
Ho Kyrios tēs eirēnēs [301]

---

[299] Source Unknown.
[300] Judg. 6:24 (KJV uses the name Jehovah Shalom).
[301] 2 Thess. 3:16.

Yahweh-Shalom was first used by Gideon when the angel of the Lord appeared to him at Ophrah in the Book of Judges, Chapter 6.

The Hebrew word *shalom* refers mostly to a person being uninjured, safe, whole, and sound. While the concept of *shalom* means wholeness, completeness, finished, perfection, safety, or wellness, the authentic, legitimate state of *shalom* comes from living in harmony with God.

In modern Israel, *shalom* is an expression of greeting or farewell. Saying *shalom* to someone is more than simply saying "Hello," or "Have a good day." Greeting someone with the word *shalom* is an expression of hope that the person being greeted may be well in every sense of the word—content, satisfied, successful, healthy, and at peace with themselves, with others, and especially with God.

The New Testament expresses *shalom* as a reconciliation of all things to God through Jesus Christ: "For God was pleased... through him [Christ] to reconcile all things to himself by making peace through the blood of his cross—through him, whether things on earth or things in heaven." [302]

---

[302] Col. 1:19, 20.

Essentially, *shalom* is a covenant, an expression of God's faithful relationship with His people.

Yahweh Shalom is a title rather than a name of God. At various junctures throughout the Old Testament, God distinguishes Himself from the false gods of neighboring nations by making His presence known in Israel. [303] Jehovah always has been deeply devoted to the good of His covenant people and He actively affirmed, pursued, and retained an intimate relationship with Israel. Despite all this, the children of Israel grew weary of their difficult circumstances and the threat of surrounding nations. In their fear, the Israelites often forgot God's miracles and dismissed His promises to them. Their fear and forgetfulness were the precursors to the sins that eventually separated them from God's presence.

In Gideon's time, the children of Israel were living under conditions of constant terror and trepidation. The Midianites, a once defeated enemy, had reemerged, plundering Israel with fierce and overwhelming brutality. Raiders from Midian overpowered Israel, forcing them to hide in caves in the surrounding hillsides. Fearful of attack and worried about the safety of their families, the Israelites hid in dens "in the mountains and the caves and the

---

[303] See Zep. 3:17.

strongholds." [304] Despair and desperation were widespread as the entire nation dwelt in fear.

Gideon was not immune from the distress and anxiety that had engulfed Israel. A simple farmer who, despite the attacks on Israel, still needed to feed his family, Gideon ventured out of the caves, down to the fields to thresh wheat. Judges 6 states that he hid out near a winepress in fear for his life. Wheat was usually threshed in an open area by oxen pulling threshing sledges over the stalks, not in the confines of a winepress. Threshing in the winepress suggests not only a mere trifle of a harvest, but also an overwhelming fear of detection by the enemy.

The Matthew Henry Commentary describes Gideon's feelings and fear: "distressed; he was threshing his wheat, not in the proper place, but by the wine-press, in some private, unsuspected corner, for fear of the Midianites."

Suddenly he became aware of a presence. "The angel of the Lord appeared to him and said, 'Mighty hero, the Lord is with you!'" [305]

An angel of the Lord appeared to Gideon, commissioning him to lead Israel and deliver them from

---

[304] Jud. 6:2.
[305] Jud. 6:12 (NLT).

the Midianites. The Biblical version of Gideon's calling and commission states:

"The Israelites did evil in the Lord's sight. So the Lord handed them over to the Midianites for seven years.

"The Midianites were so cruel that the Israelites made hiding places for themselves in the mountains, caves, and strongholds.

"Whenever the Israelites planted their crops, marauders from Midian, Amalek, and the people of the east would attack Israel,

"camping in the land and destroying crops as far away as Gaza. They left the Israelites with nothing to eat, taking all the sheep, goats, cattle, and donkeys.

"These enemy hordes, coming with their livestock and tents, were as thick as locusts; they arrived on droves of camels too numerous to count. And they stayed until the land was stripped bare.

"So Israel was reduced to starvation by the Midianites. Then the Israelites cried out to the Lord for help.

"When they cried out to the Lord because of Midian,

"the Lord sent a prophet to the Israelites. He said, "This is what the Lord, the God of Israel, says: I brought you up out of slavery in Egypt.

"I rescued you from the Egyptians and from all who oppressed you. I drove out your enemies and gave you their land.

"I told you, 'I am the Lord your God. You must not worship the gods of the Amorites, in whose land you now live.' But you have not listened to me."

The Lord reminded Israel that He had been with the Israelites throughout every stage of their journey, and He was with them still.

"Then the angel of the Lord came and sat beneath the great tree at Ophrah, which belonged to Joash of the clan of Abiezer. Gideon, the son of Joash, was threshing wheat at the bottom of a winepress to hide the grain from the Midianites.

"The angel of the Lord appeared to him and said, 'Mighty hero, the Lord is with you!'"

Gideon probably saw nothing of a mighty hero in himself at that moment as he desperately attempted to avoid detection from his enemies.

"Sir," Gideon replied, "if the Lord is with us, why has all this happened to us? And where are all the miracles our ancestors told us about? Didn't they say,

'The Lord brought us up out of Egypt'? But now the Lord has abandoned us and handed us over to the Midianites."

Gideon questions God's messenger about the desperate times that his people are experiencing.

"Then the Lord turned to him and said, "Go with the strength you have, and rescue Israel from the Midianites. I am sending you!

"'But Lord,' Gideon replied, 'how can I rescue Israel? My clan is the weakest in the whole tribe of Manasseh, and I am the least in my entire family!'"

Gideon voices his reservations. The Midianites were barbaric terrorists, massive nomadic invaders of impressive strength.

"The Lord said to him, 'I will be with you. And you will destroy the Midianites as if you were fighting against one man.'"

God was with Gideon and Israel in the present and He would be with them in the trials and battles to come. When Gideon witnesses the evidence of God's power and receives the promise of God with faith, Gideon's heart is changed, and he cries out:

"Oh, Sovereign Lord, I'm doomed! I have seen the angel of the Lord face to face!"

As the Lord had strengthened Joshua on the eve of entering the Promised Land, [306] the Lord also encouraged Gideon:

"It is all right," the Lord replied. "Do not be afraid. You will not die."

"And Gideon built an altar to the Lord there and named it *Yahweh-Shalom* (which means "the Lord is peace"). The altar remains in Ophrah in the land of the clan of Abiezer to this day." [307]

The resonant Hebrew word *shalom* reveals a state of wholeness, serenity, and satisfaction. Gideon's altar was a tribute and reminder of the Lord's provision and promise of peace. The Bible promises:

"You will keep in perfect peace those whose minds are steadfast, because they trust in you." [308]

Peace comes to us when we focus our lives on God and trust in Him. God can give us the peace that passes our own understanding. Gideon learned this when surrounded by a fierce enemy. Nothing about his time seemed peaceful, but God, strong and faithful, delivered Israel from those fear-filled days.

---

[306] See Josh. 1:9.
[307] See Jud. 2:1-24 (NLT).
[308] Isa. 26:3.

God brings calm in times of chaos—stability during times of struggle. When we trust in Him, we find comfort and calm through our worst storms, struggles, and battles. In our times of greatest darkness, we see just how true this is. Even during spiritual lapses, forgetfulness, and unfaithfulness, God never abandons us. He is always near to provide for our needs, [309] to protect us from those who wish us harm, [310] and to remind us of His prevailing love. [311]

The Lord offers us shelter from the storms of life. When circumstances are chaotic and confusing, He gives peace beyond comprehension. He is our shelter and our shield. [312] When the Israelites kept their eyes on the Lord, obeyed His commands, and held on to His promises, they found peace in His presence.

Shalom is not simply an absence of noise or strife. The word *shalom* speaks of wholeness and harmony with oneself and others, and of completion and fulfillment. As Jesus said, it is a peace far beyond the world's peace. [313]

Do you feel welcomed into a place of peace? Scripture declares that "Jesus Christ is the same

---

[309] See Ps. 81:10; 10:3.
[310] See Isa. 41:10: Ps. 18:2.
[311] See Isa. 54:10.
[312] Jud. 6:24.
[313] See John 14:27; 16:33.

yesterday, today, and forever." [314] The power of *Yahweh Shalom* and the peace He offers are very much present and available to us today. *Shalom* is possible in any situation when we choose to live by faith. A serenity exists that will allow us to rise above the panicky situations of life's circumstances that would rob us of the peace of God.

God invites us to come to Him. God is always true to His promises. He is faithful to provide an abundance of peace to all who call upon His name and choose to abide in His presence. He says: "Be still, and know that I am God; I will be exalted among the nations, I will be exalted in the earth." [315] In Him, we can find renewed peace.

Jesus doesn't want us to live in fear. He knew that His followers, both present and future, would face challenges and dangers in their lives, but He promises: "Peace I leave with you; My peace I give to you; not as the world gives do I give to you. Do not let your heart be troubled, nor let it be fearful." [316]

Feeling restless, troubled or uncertain is quite normal, but in a world where people are increasingly overwhelmed by stress, conflict, depression, anxiety, and financial, emotional, and physical uncertainty, the

---

[314] Heb. 13:8.
[315] Ps. 46:10 (NIV).
[316] John 14:27.

presence of Jehovah *Shalom* provides a peace that passes all understanding. [317] Peace is the antithesis of fear. It provides perspective, encourages hope, builds confidence, inspires courage, and affirms trust in the power of God.

Jesus invites us to find a place to retreat into the presence of God by meditating on His word and committing ourselves and our circumstances to Him. When we are consistently immersed in the presence of God and rely on Him for strength, we bear the fruit of peace in our lives. [318]

All who are filled with fear, anxiety, doubt, stress, or uncertainty can trust that Jehovah *Shalom* cares for them and will never leave them. We cannot control the uncertainties and circumstances of life, but in the presence of Jehovah *Shalom*, we can find hope, joy, strength, and peace to face each day. Despite Gideon's protestations of inadequacy, God chose him to lead Israel to victory. Like Gideon, with God by our side, we can accomplish the impossible.

"I pray that out of his glorious riches he may strengthen you with power through his Spirit in your inner being,

---

[317] Phil. 4:6.
[318] Gal. 5:22.

"so that Christ may dwell in your hearts through faith. And I pray that you, being rooted and established in love,

"may have power, together with all the Lord's holy people, to grasp how wide and long and high and deep is the love of Christ,

"and to know this love that surpasses knowledge—that you may be filled to the measure of all the fullness of God.

"Now to him who is able to do immeasurably more than all we ask or imagine, according to his power that is at work within us,

"to him be glory in the church and in Christ Jesus throughout all generations, for ever and ever! Amen." [319]

The ultimate peace is peace with God.

---

[319] Eph. 3:16-21 (NIV).

Chapter Eighteen

Son of Man-The Messiah

Jesus was known by many names and titles throughout the Bible, but Son of Man stands apart for several reasons. This seems to be a favorite self-designation of Jesus in the Gospels. In fact, Son of Man is the primary title Jesus used when referring to Himself. [320] The number of times we encounter this designation alone separates it from many of the other names and titles He uses.

Jesus is referred to as the Son of Man 88 times in the New Testament, more than 30 times in Matthew, 15 times in Mark, 25 times in Luke and a dozen in John. This reflects the Gospels' respective lengths more than

---

[320] See Matt. 12:32; 13:37; Luke 12:8; John 1:51.

anything else. There is no single book in the Gospels in which the title dominates. Jesus is always the one applying this title to Himself, except once, when the bystanders ask Him: "Who is this Son of Man?" [321] The only use of Son of Man in reference to Jesus, spoken by someone else, came from Stephen as he was being martyred. [322] and twice in the Book of Revelation. [323] Similar to the title Lamb of God, Son of Man has distinct significance and connotations defined by their Scriptural context.

In addition to being the Son of God, Jesus is a son of man in a kind of dual-nature intricacy. Many scholars believe that Son of Man is a title that focuses on the humanity of Christ while other titles, such as Son of God, focus on His deity.

It would seem, at first glance, an apt term to exemplify the human element of Christ's nature, the divine element being similarly designated as the Son of God. If not explicitly stated, an apparent impression is, at least, vaguely conveyed that Son of Man is a way of emphasizing Jesus' humanity, accentuating that Jesus is an individual of flesh and blood. While Jesus Christ certainly was a human being, (after all, He came "in the

---

[321] John 12:34.
[322] See Acts 7:56.
[323] See Rev. 1:13: 14:14.

flesh") [324] this common conception leads us in two distinct directions—the lofty, ideal element of humanity and the lowly, painful lot of the human condition. Scripture supports both views.

However, I believe that both these views miss the point. First of all, Son of Man is how Jesus referred to Himself *during* His earthly ministry, when no one would have questioned his humanity. God called the prophet Ezekiel "son of man" 93 times. Some believe that God was simply calling Ezekiel a human being and that the term Son of Man is nothing more than an implied expression for humanity.

Second, any attempt to construe a contrast between "Son of Man" as human and "Son of God" as divine is void and pointless since plenty of regular human beings, such as Adam, certain kings of Judah, and Christians in general are also designated as "sons of God." While the term Son of God doesn't necessarily imply a divine nature, to be "God the Son" would unquestionably require the divine nature of a deity.

Generically, the title, "Son of Man," may contrast the frailty and fragility of humanity with the omnipotence of God, or it could remind us of humanity's elevated status of children created in the image of God. It is both an exalting and a humbling title.

---

[324] 1 John 4:2.

In C. S. Lewis' *The Chronicles of Narnia*, just before crowning Prince Caspian king of Narnia, Aslan explains to him that being a son of Adam is "both honor enough to erect the head of the poorest beggar, and shame enough to bow the shoulders of the greatest emperor on earth." [325]

A view of the Old Testament scriptures in use during Jesus' day could help us better understand the meaning of the title "Son of Man."

A Sign of Humanity

Jesus' humanity is significant. He often called Himself the Son of Man in His interactions with others, but we shouldn't think that Son of Man is simply a designation of Jesus' humanity. As we will see later in this chapter, Jesus was also alluding to His role in the redemption of the world and declaring His identity as the Messiah. His ability to empathize with our weaknesses [326] and not sin [327] indicates that He alone met all the requirements to redeem humanity.

In several places throughout the Old Testament, the title "Son of Man" is used as an indication of human

---

[325] Lewis, C. S., *Prince Caspian (The Chronicles of Narnia #2)*.
[326] See Heb. 4:15.
[327] See 2 Cor. 5:21.

weakness. [328] In one instance, the God who does not lie or repent is portrayed in stark contrast with the "son of man" who performs both. [329] However, in other instances, [330] the term seems to simply be a euphemism for "human" and doesn't necessarily imply weakness or frailty.

A review of the New Testament Gospels reveals no specific connection between the title "Son of Man" and any single feature of Jesus' ministry. It seemingly appears to simply be what He calls Himself. When speaking of His preaching, His miracles, His power to forgive sin, His lordship of the Sabbath, or His impending death, the term "Son of Man" is simply Jesus' way of saying "I" or "me."

"Son of Man" is a title used almost exclusively by Jesus in reference to Himself. After the Gospels, it disappears completely. It did not continue into common Christian usage. Stephen saw "the son of man" standing at the right hand of God and in the Revelation the title appears twice: the Son of Man is standing amid the lampstands and is seated on a cloud with a sickle in his hand. But its use is not found elsewhere.

The fact that Jesus continually calls Himself something that He is never called in other Christian

---

[328] See Job 16:21; 25:6; 35:8; Isa. 51:12.
[329] See Num. 23:19.
[330] See Isa. 56:2; Jer. 50:40; 51:43.

writing provides significant substantiation that the Gospels contain the words and language actually spoken by Jesus and not, as some liberal scholars have suggested, merely early church theology recorded and alleged as coming from Jesus' mouth. The Gospels record of Jesus calling Himself something that the early church did not continue to call Him implies that He in reality used that expression Himself.

The title "Son of Man" connects Jesus in sympathy, circumstance, and destiny with all humanity. He identifies Himself as our brother, our fellow-sufferer, our advocate, and champion. Son of Man doesn't seem to have anything to do with man as a sinner, just with man as a man.

"The Son of man also came not to be ministered unto, but to minister, and to give his life as a ransom for many." [331]

The title "Son of Man" is used in conjunction with Jesus' prophetic words about His own suffering. He deeply feels the suffering of His fellow humans.

---

[331] Mark 10:45.

A Sign of Humility

"Son of Man" is a title of humility. Jesus was a humble man, an unpretentious carpenter consistently connected with humility and unassociated with the lavish lifestyles of religious or political leaders. Jesus followed the will of His Father, serving humanity as our bridge to God.

This Son of God, eternal in nature, left the glory of heaven, took on human flesh and became the Son of Man. Born in a manger, "despised and rejected by mankind," [332] He had "no place to lay his head." [333] The Son of Man ate and drank with sinners, [334] and suffered at the hands of men. [335] Willingly relinquishing the throne of Heaven for a stable in Bethlehem demonstrates the epitome of humility. [336]

Some scholars suggest "that Christ by this phrase [Son of Man] represented Himself as the head, the type, the ideal of the race." [337] Such a view could be supported Scripturally by the Lord's expression that "The Son of man is Lord even of the sabbath." [338] But

---

[332] Isa. 53:3.
[333] Luke 9:58.
[334] See Matt. 11:19.
[335] See Matt. 17:12.
[336] See Phil. 2:6-8.
[337] Stanton, Vincent Henry. *The Jewish and the Christian Messiah*.
[338] Mark 2:28.

we can also contrast that with the Savior's humbler statement that: "The foxes have holes, and the birds of the heaven have nests; but the Son of man hath not where to lay his head." [339]

In Judaism, being the firstborn son is significant. In Jewish culture the firstborn son is "redeemed" and predestined to serve as a priest. The firstborn son was also given a double portion of the inheritance. Sons were viewed in this time as being chosen and prepared with purpose to carry on the vision of the father. Jesus was chosen, prepared with purpose, and fulfilled the will of God the Father. He served humanity, much like a son serves his family, definitely defining the role of Jesus as the Son of Man.

Psalm 8 is an incomparable exposition of both the lowliness and the loftiness of human nature where the term "Son of Man" is used as an equivalent for man.

"What is man that you are mindful of him, and the son of man that you care for him?" [340]

The psalmist here is in awe that the God who created the heavens has respect and concern for the Son of Man. He informs us that God has crowned the

---

[339] Matt. 8:20.
[340] See Ps. 8:4-8 (ESV).

Son of Man with glory and honor and set Him over all God's works.

A Sign of Leadership

Jesus was unquestionably the humblest person to walk the earth. However, as mentioned earlier, Jesus did not have to contest undeserved haughty or proud perceptions imposed on Him by others. His humanity and His humility were never in question. If we examine the Psalms, we will encounter the title, "Son of Man," used in a context that indicates not human weakness but human strength. Psalms 80 is an appeal, in an age of national decline, for the establishing of a hero to redeem Israel.

"They have burned it with fire; they have cut it down; may they perish at the rebuke of your face!

"But let your hand be on the man of your right hand, the son of man whom you have made strong for yourself!

"Then we shall not turn back from you; give us life, and we will call upon your name!" [341]

The man at God's right hand most likely refers to the king of Judah. Apparently, "Son of Man" is a title

---

[341] Ps. 80:16-18.

that can appropriately be attached to a powerful and honored individual, and not just to the meek and humble.

In Hebrew culture, a firstborn son is highly esteemed and given substantial authority. He is honored and considered worthy to carry on the mission and purpose of his father. He is given authority to lead. As the Son of Man, Jesus is the leader of mankind. Seated at the right hand of God, Jesus provides us the opportunity to connect with God the Father. Christ's influence over our lives allows us to have a positive impact and effect in this world.

As the Lamb of God, Jesus was the perfect sacrifice, providing salvation for all who accept Him. As the Son of Man, Jesus is our perfect exemplar and leader. Viewing Jesus in this light allows us to see Him through the eyes of gratitude and gratitude is the root of pure worship.

The deeper we discover Jesus as our spiritual leader, the better prepared we become to approach Him in worship. As the Son of Man, we can worship Jesus as our director, our guide, and our leader. Jesus did not simply prepare a way for our salvation; He is the way. [342]

---

[342] John 14:6.

A Sign of Deity

"Son of Man" is a title of deity. The phrase, "the son of man," appears over 90 times in the book of Ezekiel. Ezekiel is called "son of man" even more frequently (93 times) than Jesus is (82 times) in all four of the gospels.

Karl Nosgen explains that the title, "Son of Man," as applied to Ezekiel "expresses the contrast between what Ezekiel is in himself and what God will make out of him, and to make his mission appear to him not as his own, but as the work of God, and thus to lift him up, whenever the flesh threatens to faint and fail." [343]

Ezekiel, the son of man, was chosen to be a prophet in Israel. Like Jesus, he was thirty years old at the time he began his ministry.

"Son of man, I send you to the people of Israel, to nations of rebels, who have rebelled against me. They and their fathers have transgressed against me to this very day... And whether they hear or refuse to hear (for they are a rebellious house) they will know that a prophet has been among them." [344]

---

[343] Nosgen, Karl Friedrich. *Christus der Menschenund Gotlessohn,* 1869 German edition.
[344] Eze. 2:3-5.

Ezekiel may have been a son of man, but Jesus is *the* Son of Man. Jesus, the Son of Man, Ezekiel, and other prophets as well, were sent to the lost sheep of Israel. They spoke only what they heard from the Father.

Ezekiel witnessed the abominations in the temple.[345] Jesus also observed abominations in the temple and drove the money changers out with a whip of cords.

Ezekiel spoke in parables.[346] Jesus also taught with parables so that Israel in their rebellion wouldn't understand him.

Ezekiel announced the destruction of Jerusalem[347] as did Jesus in the Olivet Discourse.

Ezekiel symbolically shouldered Israel's punishment.[348] Jesus in reality bore the punishment of the entire earth.

As *the* Son of Man, Jesus is the ultimate ideal and representation of all that God intends mankind to

---

[345] Eze. 8:6.
[346] Ibid. 17:2.
[347] Ibid. 9:1-11.
[348] Ibid. 4:4-8.

become, the embodiment of truth and grace. [349] In Him "all the fullness of the Deity lives in bodily form." [350]

As the Son of Man, Jesus:

Could forgive sins. [351]
Is Lord of the Sabbath. [352]
Offers salvation. [353]
Rose from the dead. [354]
Executes judgment. [355]

"I say to all of you," announced Jesus at His trial, "From now on you will see the Son of Man sitting at the right hand of the Mighty One and coming on the clouds of heaven." [356] This simple yet significant statement immediately ended the trial, as the court accused the Lord of blasphemy and condemned Him to death. [357]

---

[349] John 1:14.
[350] Col. 2:9.
[351] Matt. 9:6.
[352] Mark 2:28.
[353] Luke: 9:56; 19:10.
[354] Mark 9:9.
[355] John 6:27.
[356] Matt 26:64.
[357] Ibid. vs. 65, 66.

A Sign of Messiahship

In an apocalyptic vision, Daniel sees "one like a son of man coming with the clouds of heaven" [358] and receiving a kingdom which will never pass away. Daniel is then called a "son of man." [359] In his vision, Daniel sees four beasts coming out of the sea—a lion with eagle's wings, a bear, a four-headed leopard, and a terrible monster with ten heads. These beasts rule over the earth; but at last the kingdom is taken away from them and given to a fifth ruler:

"I saw in the night visions, and behold, with the clouds of heaven there came one like a son of man, and he came to the Ancient of Days and was presented before him.

"And to him was given dominion and glory and a kingdom, that all peoples, nations, and languages should serve him; his dominion is an everlasting dominion, which shall not pass away, and his kingdom one that shall not be destroyed." [360]

This passage in Daniel is obviously Messianic. Jesus cautioned His disciples "...not to tell anyone he was the Messiah." [361] Claiming to be the Son of Man

---

[358] See Dan. 7.
[359] Dan. 8:17.
[360] Dan. 7:13, 14 (ESV).
[361] Matt. 16:20.

gave Jesus a perfect platform for connecting with the common people. But when we compare Daniel's words with Jesus' declaration to the high priest during His trial mentioned earlier: "You will see the Son of Man seated at the right hand of Power and coming on the clouds of heaven," [362] the message of Jesus' declaration becomes clear.

When Jesus called himself the Son of Man, the knowledgeable and the spiritually inclined would have easily recognized the implication of this quiet claim of Messiahship. In Daniel, the title, "Son of Man," expresses Messiahship, and Jesus was fully conscious of His role as the Messiah.

"Then shall appear the sign of the Son of man in heaven: and then shall all the tribes of the earth mourn, and they shall see the Son of man coming on the clouds of heaven with power and great glory." [363]

Perhaps Jesus chose Son of Man as a preferred self-designation because it half concealed as well as half revealed His Messianic mission. Had Jesus gone around claiming outright to be the Messiah, He may have been crucified much earlier in His ministry. His contemporaries were not prepared for an open declaration of Himself in this character.

---

[362] Matt. 26:64 (ESV).
[363] Matt. 24:30

While the title, "Son of Man," conveyed meaning to Jesus, it did not express a Messianic claim to the public ear. As evidenced by the perplexity displayed by His listeners when they asked: "Who is this Son of man?" [364] or when Jesus asked His disciples at Caesarea Philippi: "Who do men say that the Son of man is?" [365] The title did not imply Messiah for everyone.

The author of Hebrews referred to the Son of Man mentioned in the Psalms to demonstrate to us that Jesus, the true Son of Man, will be the ruler of all things. [366] Jesus was human but He is also the Son of God.

"And a voice from Heaven said, 'This is my dearly loved Son, who brings me great joy.'" [367]

As the Son of God and the Son of Man, Jesus Christ is deserving of both titles.

---

[364] John 12:34.
[365] See Matt. 16:13-20.
[366] Hebrews 2:5–9; cf. Psalm 8:4–6
[367] Matt. 3:17.

Chapter Nineteen

Yeshua Saves!

An angel appeared to Joseph and announced that his wife Mary "will bear a son, and" that he should "call his name Jesus, for he will save his people from their sins." [368]

The truth is the angel never said to name Him Jesus. He said, "You shall call his name *Yeshua*."

The name Jesus comes from the Greek Ἰησοῦς, pronounced "Yay-soos." The Greek version of *Yeshua* was altered as it was adopted by the English language. First century Greek translations of the Bible have *Yeshua* listed as *Yesous* of which the name Jesus is

---

[368] Matt. 1:21.

derived. Jesus appears to be an English translation of the Greek version of the Hebrew name that doesn't even resemble the original name suggested by the angel.

Basically, Joshua and Jesus are the same name. Joshua is *Yeshua* translated from Hebrew into English, Jesus is *Yeshua* translated from Greek into English. The name Jesus didn't even exist during the time that Jesus Christ was on earth. It came into existence in the 4th century when it was configured by the Council of Nicea of the Roman Catholic Church. In the 1st century, the Greek name *Yesous* represented the Hebrew name *Yeshua*, a shortened form of the Hebrew *Yehoshua.*

Yehoshua is a compound name consisting of two parts: The first part is the prefix form of the Tetragram—*YHVH*, God's Four-Letter Name: *Yod-He-Vav-He*. The second part is a form of the Hebrew verb *yasha,* meaning "to deliver, save, or rescue." The name conveys the concept that God (*YHVH*) delivers or saves his people.

The name *Yeshua*, it is believed, can be found hidden within the Tetragram *YHVH*, as *Yeshua HaNazarei Vemelekh HaYehudim*, translated as, "Jesus of Nazareth, King of the Jews," similar to the familiar Latin inscription *INRI* (*Iesus Nazarenus Rex Iudaeorum*) that Pontius Pilate had nailed to Christ's cross.

Yeshua, the Hebrew word for Jesus, can be found in the Hebrew Bible and other ancient texts referenced among the Jewish faith. Hebrew is still considered the holy language for worship and prayer. *Yeshua* is Jesus Christ of the New Testament, and the Messiah who was prophesied to come in the Old Testament. It is a more personal name for Jesus because it originated in His own lifetime. The Hebrew *Yeshua* relates specifically to when Jesus resided in the presence of the Jewish nation, but how can this name feel as personal to us as the name "Jesus?"

Words for the same object are said differently across languages. A book, for example, would be *libro* in Spanish, *livre* in French, *kinha* in Czech and 书 (Shu) in Chinese. The dialect may vary, but the object itself does not. Similarly, we can refer to Jesus by different names without changing His nature.

In English, we say Jesus with a J that sounds like "gee." The Portuguese pronounce Jesus with a J that sounds like "geh," and Spanish speakers call him Jesus with a J that sounds like "hey." Jesus, Joshua, *Yeshua* and *Yesous* all mean "to save or deliver." How the Messiah's name is translated is not essential to salvation.

Those who are fluent in Hebrew, Greek, and Aramaic would decipher *Yeshua* as "deliverer, savior," and realize that the man we call Jesus was more than just a man. To them, the name Jesus would sound so gentile, making His role as Messiah all the less recognizable. But when Jewish people hear His name in Hebrew, there is a Scriptural and historical recognition. The name *Yeshua* was known and used in Jewish history, and it means "salvation" to Jewish ears.

Also, associating Jesus of the New Testament with Joshua, the son of Nun, of the Old Testament, we would see the emerging similarities of both *Yeshuas* leading the people out of bondage in Egypt, standing with them through their trials in the desert, and offering salvation by bringing them into a new, promised land. For us, *Yeshua* shows that He has always been the deliverer and rescuer of people in need.

Sadly, so much suffering and persecution has been inflicted upon the Jewish people in the name of Jesus that He has become a stumbling block and an offense to them, and now is often considered an enemy of the Jewish people. Jews do not recognize Jesus as the Messiah; consequently, they do not say *Yeshua* but *Yeshu.*

In Israel, Jesus is perceived as a gentile and a Christian. But Jesus wasn't Christian. He wasn't a follower of Christ—He was *the* Christ, the Jewish Messiah! Jesus wasn't Christian, Mary wasn't Catholic, and John wasn't Baptist: They were all Jewish! The word

Christ is Greek for Messiah, so Jesus Christ literally means: *Yeshua* the Messiah.

Joseph dressed in strange Egyptian clothing, speaking a foreign language, went undetected by his brothers when they came seeking assistance. For centuries now *Yeshua* has been bringing salvation to the gentiles and consequently appears shrouded in gentile terms and culture, making it difficult for His Jewish brothers and sisters to recognize Him as one of them. Joseph was a foreshadowing of the Messiah—sold for silver, suffering at the hands of his brothers, and yet procuring salvation both for his family and for others. This truth will eventually reach the Jewish nation as God promised:

"I will pour out on the house of David and the inhabitants of Jerusalem a spirit of grace and pleas for mercy, so that, when they look on me, on him whom they have pierced, they shall mourn for him, as one mourns for an only child, and weep bitterly over him, as one weeps over a firstborn." [369]

Yeshua is one name we cannot properly ignore. Jesus would have gone by the Hebrew version of His name. The significance of Christ being called *Yeshua* is evident. He is our Lord and Savior, the one who achieved the purposes of God, suffering for our sins

---

[369] Zech. 12:10.

and redemption, then dying on the cross. *Yeshua* is a name that represents Jesus' Hebrew identity and establishes a stronger connection with believers of all generations.

To modern Christianity, the name *Yeshua* does not carry the same significance as the name Jesus and yet, it is a name that celebrates all that Christ accomplished on earth and in heaven for those who profess His existence. The name *Yeshua* establishes the bond we have with the Messiah in acknowledging that He delivered us from evil bondage and saved us from our sinful natures. It strengthens our awareness of Him with a perspective that is not shaped by any religious organization, but from the setting in which He arrived on this planet.

His mother knew him as *Yeshua* rather than Jesus, but God doesn't give preeminence to one language over another. We are not commanded to call upon the name of the Lord exclusively in Hebrew. Nor does it matter how we pronounce His name.

Yahweh is a name of authority and great power. It says to all who are willing to hear: "I AM the one true God, follow me." Jesus Christ, the great I AM, didn't just exist thousands of years ago when all these marvelous names were first revealed. He is undeniably as present today and He loves us with an incomprehensible love. He is still the great I AM because He never changes and we can trust His loving leadership in our own lives, just as Moses trusted Him to lead the children of Israel. He calls us for His specific purposes, reminding us that He knows the way and He has a plan.

"And it shall come to pass that everyone who calls upon the name of the Lord shall be saved." [370]

God knows who calls on His name, whether in English, Portuguese, Spanish, Chinese, French, or Hebrew. Jesus Christ is still the same Lord and Savior. Call on His name. His power does not come from how we pronounce His name, but from the person who bears that name: our Lord and Savior, Jesus Christ.

---

[370] Acts 2:21 (ESV).

Chapter Twenty

The God Ēl

Ēl Bethel: The God of the House of God.

"He built an altar there, and called the place *Ēl-bethel*, because there God had revealed Himself to him when he fled from his brother." [371]

Ēlohim Chaseddi: The God of My Mercy.

"My God (*Ēlohim*) in His lovingkindness (*Chaseddi*) will meet me; God will let me look triumphantly upon my foes." [372]

---

[371] Gen. 35:7.
[372] Ps. 59:10.

Ēl Ēlohe Yisrael: The mighty God of Israel.

"Then he erected there an altar and called it *Ēl-Ēlohe-Israel*." [373]

Ēl Emunah: The Faithful God.

"Know therefore that the Lord your God is God; he is the faithful God (*Ēl Emunah*), keeping his covenant of love to a thousand generations of those who love him and keep his commandments." [374]

Ēlohei Tehillati: God of My Praise.

"My God (*Ēlohei*), whom I praise (*Tehillati*), do not remain silent." [375]

Ēl Hakabodh: The God of Glory.

"The voice of the Lord is over the waters; the God of glory (*Ēl Hakabodh*) thunders, the Lord thunders over the mighty waters." [376]

---

[373] Gen 33:20.
[374] Deut. 7:9.
[375] Ps. 109:1.
[376] Ps. 29:3.

Ēlohim Chayim: The Living God.

"This is how you will know that the living God (*Ēlohim Chayim*) is among you..." [377]

Ēl Hayyay: God of My Life.

"By day the Lord directs his love, at night his song is with me —a prayer to the God (*Ēl*) of my life (*Hayyay*). [378]

Ēlohim Kedoshim: Holy God.

"Joshua said to the people, 'You are not able to serve the Lord. He is a holy God (*Ēlohim Kedoshim*); he is a jealous God. He will not forgive your rebellion and your sins.'" [379]

Ēl Kanna: Jealous God.

"You shall not bow down to them or worship them; for I, the Lord your God, am a jealous God (*Ēl Kanna*), punishing the children for the sin of the

---

[377] Josh. 3:10.
[378] Ps. 42:8.
[379] Josh. 24:19.

parents to the third and fourth generation of those who hate me." [380]

    Ēlohei Ma'uzzi: God of My Strength.

"God (*Ēlohei*) is my strong (*Ma'uzzi*) fortress; And He sets the blameless in His way." [381]

    Ēlohim Machase Lanu: God Our Refuge.

"Trust in him at all times, you people; pour out your hearts to him, for God (*Ēlohim*) is our refuge (*Machase Lanu*)." [382]

    Ēli Maelekhi: God My King.

"Your procession, God, has come into view, the procession of my God and King (*Ēli Maelekhi*) into the sanctuary." [383]

---

[380] Exo. 20:5.
[381] 2 Sam. 22:33.
[382] Ps. 62:8.
[383] Ps. 68:24.

Ēl Nekamoth: God that Avenges.

"He is the God (*Ēl*) who avenges (*Nekamoth*) me, who subdues nations under me." [384]

Ēlohenu Olam: Our Everlasting God.

"For this God is our God for ever and ever (*Ēlohenu Olam*); he will be our guide even to the end." [385]

Ēlohim Ozer Li: God My Helper.

"Surely God is my help (*Ēlohim Ozer Li*); the Lord is the one who sustains me." [386]

Ēl Sali: God, My Rock.

"The Lord lives, and blessed be my rock (*Ēl Sali*); and exalted be God, the rock of my salvation." [387]

---

[384] Ps. 18:47.
[385] Ps. 48:14.
[386] Ps. 54:4.
[387] 2 Sam. 22:47.

Ēlohim Shophtim Ba-arets: God that Judges in the earth.

"Then people will say, 'Surely the righteous still are rewarded; surely there is a God who judges the earth (*Ēlohim Shophtim Ba-arets*).'" [388]

Ēl Simchath Gili: God My Exceeding Joy.

"Then I will go to the altar of God, to God, my joy and my delight (*Ēl Simchath Gili*). I will praise you with the lyre, O God, my God." [389]

Ēlohim Tsebaoth: God of Hosts.

"Restore us, God Almighty (*Ēlohim Tsebaoth*); make your face shine on us, that we may be saved." [390]

Ēlohe Tishuathi: God of My Salvation.

"Deliver me from the guilt of bloodshed, O God, you who are God my Savior (*Ēlohe Tishuathi*), and my tongue will sing of your righteousness." [391]

---

[388] Ps. 58:11.
[389] Ps. 43:4.
[390] Ps. 80:7.
[391] Ps. 51:14.

Ēlohe Tsadeki: God of My Righteousness.

"Answer me when I call to you, my righteous God (*Ēlohe Tsadeki*). Give me relief from my distress; have mercy on me and hear my prayer." [392]

Ēlohei Yakob: God of Jacob.

"May the Lord answer you when you are in distress; may the name of the God of Jacob (*Ēlohei Yakob*) protect you." [393]

Ēlohei Marom: God of Heights.

"With what shall I come to the Lord and bow myself before the God (*Ēlohei*) on high (*Marom*)? Shall I come to Him with burnt offerings, with yearling calves?" [394]

Ēlohei Mikkarov: God Who is Near.

"Am I a God (*Ēlohei*) who is near (*Mikkarov*), declares the Lord, and not a God far off?" [395]

---

[392] Ps. 4:1.
[393] Ps. 20:1.
[394] Mic. 6:6.
[395] Jer. 23:23.

Ēlohei Haelohim: The God of Gods.

"For the Lord your God is the God of gods (*Ēlohei Haelohim*) and the Lord of lords, the great, the mighty, and the awesome God who does not show partiality nor take a bribe." [396]

Ēlohei Chasdi: God of My Kindness.

"O my strength, I will sing praises to You; For God is my stronghold, the God (*Ēlohim*) who shows me lovingkindness (*Chasdi*)." [397]

Ēlohim Bashamayim: God in Heaven

"When we heard it, our hearts melted and no courage remained in any man any longer because of you; for the Lord your God, He is God (*Ēlohim*) in heaven (Bashamayim) above and on earth beneath." [398]

---

[396] Duet. 10:17.
[397] Ps. 59:17.
[398] Josh. 2:11.

Ēl-Gibhor: Mighty God.

"For unto us a child is born, to us a son is given; and the government shall be on his shoulder: and his name shall be called Wonderful, Counselor, Mighty God (*Ēl-Gibhor*), Everlasting Father, Prince of Peace." [399]

Ēl-Olam: The Everlasting God.

"Do you not know? Have you not heard? The Lord is an eternal God (*Ēl-Olam*), the creator of the earth. He does not get tired or weary; there is no limit to his wisdom." [400]

Ēl-Chuwl: The God who Gave Birth.

"How difficult it is for me to fathom your thoughts about me, O God! (*Ēl-Chuwl*) How vast is their sum total!" [401]

---

[399] Isa. 9:6 (WEB).
[400] Isa. 40:28-31.
[401] Ps. 139:13-18.

Ēl-Deah: God of Knowledge.

"Do not keep talking so proudly or let your mouth speak such arrogance, for the Lord is a God who knows (*Ēl-Deah*), and by him deeds are weighed. [402]

Attiyq Youm: The Ancient of Days.

"As I looked, thrones were placed, and the Ancient of Days (*Attiyq Youm*) took his seat; his clothing was white as snow, and the hair of his head like pure wool; his throne was fiery flames; its wheels were burning fire." [403]

Immanuel: God with Us

"Therefore the Lord Himself will give you a sign: Behold, a virgin will be with child and bear a son, and she will call His name *Immanuel*." [404]

---

[402] 1 Sam. 2:3.
[403] Dan 7:9.
[404] Isa. 7:14.

Go'el: Kinsman Redeemer

"In Your lovingkindness You have led the people whom You have redeemed (*Go'el*); In Your strength You have guided them to Your holy habitation." [405]

Kadosh: The Holy One

"'To whom then will you liken Me that I would be his equal?' says the Holy One (*Kadosh*)." [406]

Ruach Ēlohim: The Spirit of God

"When they came to the hill there, behold, a group of prophets met him; and the Spirit of God (*Ruach Ēlohim*) came upon him mightily, so that he prophesied among them." [407]

'Ab: Father

"A father (*'Ab*) of the fatherless and a judge for the widows, Is God in His holy habitation." [408]

---

[405] Exo. 15:13.
[406] Isa. 40:25.
[407] 1 Sam. 10:10
[408] Ps. 68:5.

'Or Goyim: Light of the Nations

"I am the Lord, I have called You in righteousness, I will also hold You by the hand and watch over You, And I will appoint You as a covenant to the people, As a light to the nations (*'Or Goyim*)." [409]

---

[409] Isa. 42:6.

Chapter Twenty-one

Jehovah – Our God

Yahweh-Shammah: The Lord is present.

"The circumference of the city will be six miles. The name of the city from that day forward will be: 'The LORD Is There (*Yahweh-Shammah*).'" [410]

Jehovah Maginnenu: The LORD Our Defense.

"Indeed, our shield (*Maginnenu*) belongs to the Lord (*Jehovah*), our king to the Holy One of Israel." [411]

---

[410] Eze. 48:35.
[411] Ps.89:18.

Jehovah Adon Kol Ha-arets: The LORD, the Lord of All the Earth.

"See, the ark of the covenant of the Lord of all the earth (*Jehovah Adon Kol Ha-arets*) will go into the Jordan ahead of you." [412]

Jehovah Chereb: The LORD, the Sword.

"Blessed are you, Israel! Who is like you, a people saved by the Lord (*Jehovah*)? He is your shield and helper and your glorious sword (*Chereb*). Your enemies will cower before you, and you will tread on their heights." [413]

Jehovah Tsaba: LORD of Hosts.

"Then David said to the Philistine, 'You come to me with a sword, a spear, and a javelin, but I come to you in the name of the Lord of hosts (*Jehovah Tsaba*), the God of the armies of Israel, whom you have taunted.'" [414]

---

[412] Josh. 3:11.
[413] Duet. 33:29.
[414] 1 Sam. 17:45.

Jehovah Gibbor Milchamah: The LORD Mighty in Battle.

"Who is this King of glory? The Lord strong and mighty, the Lord mighty in battle (*Jehovah Gibbor Milchamah*)." [415]

Jehovah Goelekh: The LORD Thy Redeemer.

"You will drink the milk of nations and be nursed at royal breasts. Then you will know that I, the Lord (*Jehovah*), am your Savior, your Redeemer (*Goelekh*), the Mighty One of Jacob." [416]

Jehovah Ēl Ēlohim: The LORD God of Gods.

"The Mighty One, God, the Lord (*Jehovah*), the Mighty One (*Ēl*), God (*Ēlohim*), the Lord! He knows, and may Israel itself know. If it was in rebellion, or if in an unfaithful act against the Lord do not save us this day!" [417]

---

[415] Ps. 24:8.
[416] Isa. 60:16.
[417] Josh. 22:22.

Jehovah Ēlohim: The LORD God.

"This is the account of the heavens and the earth when they were created, in the day that the Lord (*Jehovah*) God (*Ēlohim*) made earth and heaven." [418]

Jehovah Ēlohim Ab: The LORD God of Your Forefathers.

"So Joshua said to the sons of Israel, "How long will you put off entering to take possession of the land which the Lord (*Jehovah*), the God (*Ēlohim*) of your fathers (*Ab*), has given you?" [419]

Jehovah Ēl Ēlyon: The LORD, the Most High God.

"Abram said to the king of Sodom, 'I have sworn to the Lord (*Jehovah*) God (*Ēl*) Most High (*Ēlyon*), possessor of heaven and earth.'" [420]

---

[418] Gen. 2:4.
[419] Josh. 18:3.
[420] Gen. 14:22.

Jehovah Ēl Emeth: LORD God of Truth.

"Into Your hand I commit my spirit; You have ransomed me, O Lord (*Jehovah*), God (*Ēl*) of truth (*Emeth*)." [421]

Jehovah Ēl Gemuwal: The LORD God of Recompense.

"For the destroyer is coming against her, against Babylon, And her mighty men will be captured, Their bows are shattered; For the Lord (*Jehovah*) is a God (*Ēl*) of recompense (*Gemuwal*), He will fully repay." [422]

Jehovah Ēlohim Tsaba: LORD God of Hosts.

"You, O Lord (*Jehovah*) God (*Ēlohim*) of hosts (*Tsaba*), the God of Israel, Awake to punish all the nations; Do not be gracious to any who are treacherous in iniquity." [423]

---

[421] Ps. 31:5.
[422] Jer. 51:56.
[423] Ps. 59:5.

Jehovah Hashopet: The LORD the Judge.

"I have not wronged you, but you are doing me wrong by waging war against me. Let the Lord (*Jehovah*), the Judge (*Hashopet*), decide the dispute this day between the Israelites and the Ammonites." [424]

Jehovah Immeka: The LORD Is with You.

"When the angel of the Lord appeared to Gideon, he said, "The Lord (*Jehovah*) is with you (*Immeka*), mighty warrior." [425]

Sar Shalom: Prince of Peace.

"For a child will be born to us, a son will be given to us; and the government will rest on His shoulders; and His name will be called Wonderful Counselor, Mighty God, Eternal Father, Prince of Peace (*Sar Shalom*)." [426]

---

[424] Jud. 11:27.
[425] Jud. 6:12.
[426] Isa. 9:6.

Jehovah Kanna Shemo: The LORD Whose Name Is Jealous.

"Do not worship any other god, for the Lord (*Jehovah*), whose name (*Shemo*) is Jealous (*Kanna*), is a jealous God." [427]

Jehovah Machsi: The LORD My Refuge.

"If you say, 'The Lord (*Jehovah*) is my refuge (*Machsi*),' and you make the Most High your dwelling." [428]

Jehovah Magen: The LORD My Shield.

"Blessed are you, Israel! Who is like you, a people saved by the Lord (*Jehovah*)? He is your shield (*Magen*) and helper and your glorious sword. Your enemies will cower before you, and you will tread on their heights." [429]

---

[427] Exo. 34:14.
[428] Ps. 91:9.
[429] Duet. 33:29.

Jehovah Mauzzi: The LORD My Fortress.

"Lord (*Jehovah*), my strength and my fortress (*Mauzzi*), my refuge in time of distress, to you the nations will come from the ends of the earth and say, 'Our ancestors possessed nothing but false gods, worthless idols that did them no good.'" [430]

Jehovah Ha-Melech: The LORD the King.

"With trumpets and the blast of the ram's horn—shout for joy before the Lord (*Jehovah*) the King (*Ha-Melech*)." [431]

Peleh Yo'etz: Wonderful Counselor

"For unto us a Child is born, Unto us a Son is given; and the government will be upon His shoulder. And His name will be called Wonderful (*Peleh*), Counselor (*Yo'etz*), Mighty God, Everlasting Father, Prince of Peace." [432]

---

[430] Jer. 16:19.
[431] Ps. 98:6.
[432] Isa. 9:6.

Jehovah Mephalti: The LORD My Deliverer.

"The Lord (*Jehovah*) is my rock, my fortress and my deliverer (*Mephalti*); my God is my rock, in whom I take refuge, my shield and the horn of my salvation, my stronghold." [433]

Jehovah Metsudhathi: The LORD My High Tower.

"The Lord (*Jehovah*) is my rock, my fortress (*Metsudhathi*) and my deliverer; my God is my rock, in whom I take refuge, my shield and the horn of my salvation, my stronghold." [434]

Jehovah Moshiekh: The LORD Your Savior.

"I will make your oppressors eat their own flesh; they will be drunk on their own blood, as with wine. Then all mankind will know that I, the Lord (*Jehovah*), am your Savior (*Moshiekh*), your Redeemer, the Mighty One of Jacob." [435]

---

[433] Ps. 18:2.
[434] Ibid.
[435] Isa. 49:26.

Jehovah Ori: The LORD My Light.

"The Lord (*Jehovah*) is my light (*Ori*) and my salvation—whom shall I fear? The Lord is the stronghold of my life—of whom shall I be afraid?" [436]

Jehovah Sal'I: The LORD My Rock.

"The Lord (*Jehovah*) is my rock (*Sal'I*), my fortress and my deliverer; my God is my rock, in whom I take refuge, my shield and the horn of my salvation, my stronghold." [437]

Jehovah Tsidkenu: The LORD Our Righteousness.

"In his days Judah will be saved and Israel will live in safety. This is the name by which he will be called: The Lord (*Jehovah*) Our Righteous (*Tsidkenu*) Savior." [438]

---

[436] Ps. 27:1.
[437] Ps. 18:2.
[438] Jer. 23:6.

Jehovah Malakh: The Angel of the Lord.

"Now the angel of the Lord (*Jehovah Malakh*) found her by a spring of water in the wilderness, by the spring on the way to Shur." [439]

Jehovah Hoshiah: O LORD Save.

"Lord (*Jehovah*), give victory (*Hoshiah*) to the king! Answer us when we call!" [440]

Jehovah Tsemach: The Branch of the Lord.

"In that day the Branch of the Lord (*Jehovah Tsemach*) will be beautiful and glorious, and the fruit of the earth will be the pride and the adornment of the survivors of Israel." [441]

Esh Oklah: A Consuming Fire.

"For the Lord your God is a consuming fire (*Esh Oklah*), a jealous God." [442]

---

[439] Gen. 16:7.
[440] Ps. 20:9.
[441] Isa. 4:2.
[442] Duet. 4:24.

Chapter Twenty-two

Praise His Name

The Duke of Wellington was once asked what he would have done differently in his life. He did not say he would change the way he fought the magnificent Battle of Waterloo—or any other battle. He simply said, "I should have given more praise."

We all want to be accepted and appreciated. Unfortunately, many go through their days never hearing a kind word, an encouraging comment, or the faintest expression of praise. Sincere praise can be such a sustaining force in our lives. Words of praise and feelings of commendation are seldom forgotten.

We have the privilege of honorably and righteously bearing the name of God and, when we do, we walk in His light. God can be a source of comfort and hope in times of affliction and despair, like a balm for the troubled soul. We are blessed that this source of divine understanding and empathy exists.

God can, of course, sustain us through our sorrows but He can also sustain us through good times. Our nature is generally to think of the Lord more in times of need than in times when things are going well. If we see God only as a comfort in our afflictions, we limit His glory and grandeur and divine character.

God is the source of joy, the source of goodness, the source of beauty. All that is right in the universe is because of Him and His divine plan. If we exclude Him from the good and pleasant experiences of our lives, we limit our understanding of God and His relationship with us. God "has made everything beautiful in his time." [443]

When we love God with all our heart, might, mind, and strength, we surrender our intellect to God. Comparatively, more knees are bent in reverence to God than minds. Our praise should proceed from the whole soul, because of the dawning realization of all that God has done, is doing, and will yet do for all His children as well as for us personally.

---

[443] Eccl. 3:11.

More people, it would seem, tend to partially keep the second great commandment than to truly keep the first. But it is the first great commandment that sets the tone and enables the second to be "like unto" it. We can have an understanding heart and a humble spirit to reach out and lift others. Any good and worthy work can be a hallowed offering unto His holy name.

When we speak of praising God, we are addressing more than ritualistic incantations or merely saying good things about God. We should use our best gifts, talents, and energies to show our gratitude to God and to include Him in all the good in our lives. God does not want our superficial invocations but a heartfelt awareness of our relationship to Him. The more specific and frequent our praise, the better.

For myself, I often wonder: Have I praised Him enough today? Have I thanked Him for the small successes I have achieved? Even when I have, have I specifically and genuinely given the honor and the glory to Him? If we are meek, we will see the complete range of God's goodness in our lives. We will feel the depth of His love and we will experience the manifestations of His kindness.

God has so carefully revealed Himself and His character to us through His numerous descriptive names in Scripture. Our task is to search and ponder these instructive insights, and then to apply these revelations developmentally and personally. Knowing what God is like is as vital as our knowing that He lives!

Discovering God's attributes through the revelation of His names draws us closer to Him and can lead us to repentance. [444]

"I have loved you with an everlasting love; I have drawn you with unfailing kindness." [445]

His tender care, including His guiding hand in micro-matters of daily life are constantly demonstrated and attested. We should acknowledge His hand not only in the governance of the galaxies but also in the management and direction of the miniscule details of our lives.

We can praise His timing as well as His purposes, even when our tactical situations are stress-filled, and like Moses, we teeter at the edge of a tempestuous sea. When we feel like the anxious young man with Elisha surrounded by the enemy's horses and chariots, we can best praise Christ by taking His hand firmly and constantly!

Our praise may begin with merely the acknowledgment of Christ, then ripen into real appreciation, followed by deep admiration, and on to

---

[444] See Rom. 2:4.
[445] Jer. 31:3.

genuine adoration until, finally, it blossoms into reverent emulation. Our ultimate praise is to pattern our lives after Jesus'.

All that is ultimately required to partake of God's joy is a sensitive soul. All that is required to give praise and gratitude to Him is to love Him and each other.

No wonder we will praise the name of God "forever and ever."

Chapter Twenty-three

Taking On His Name

One name above all others brings joy to the desolate heart. One name falls in hushed and hallowed tones from the lips of angels. One name speaks peace to the sorrowing soul. One name leads true believers to glory everlasting. Only one name; the name of the one sent to bring salvation, the name of the one who ransomed us from Satan's grasp. Except for the name of the Almighty Elohim, Jesus of Nazareth is that one name above every other name on earth or in heaven.[446] As Christians, our willingness to take on us the name of Jesus Christ has significant meaning.

---

[446] See Phil. 2:9-11.

Whenever we publicly proclaim our belief in Jesus Christ, we take His name on us. As Christians, we are given countless opportunities to proclaim our belief to friends, neighbors, co-workers, and acquaintances. Peter tells us that we should "sanctify Christ as Lord in your hearts, always being ready to make a defense to everyone who asks you to give an account for the hope that is in you, but with gentleness and respect." [447]

As God placed His name on Christ, [448] Jesus made His words and actions those of His Father. He spoke for His Father, using the first person, as though He *were* the Almighty Elohim. We should also speak and behave appropriately when witnessing in the name of Deity. Jesus is God, and God works miracles in His own right; He needs neither the name nor the power of another. Those of us who call ourselves Christians, in contrast, act and operate under the name above all other names, the name of our Lord and Savior. [449]

As Christians, we are compelled to serve Jesus. The name of the Lord seems to be Scripturally linked to the work of His kingdom. Paul addressed certain Christians who had ministered to others, saying that the Lord would not forget the labor of love they had

---

[447] 1 Pet. 3:15 (NASB).
[448] See John 5:43; 10:25.
[449] See Eph. 3:15; Phil. 2:9.

"shown toward His name." [450] When Peter, along with other apostles were beaten, they rejoiced "that they were counted worthy to suffer dishonor for the name." [451] Our willingness to be called Christians, to act in the name of Jesus Christ, demonstrates our willingness to work for His kingdom.

When we take on the name of Jesus, we can look forward to incomprehensible blessings that will be given to those called by His name at the last day. When we demonstrate faith in the sacred name of Jesus Christ, we qualify by faith to have our sins borne by the Lord. In spiritual terms, we become the sons and daughters of Christ, heirs to His kingdom. These are they who will be called by His name in the last day.

True Christians choose to do things the Lord's way. They willingly surrender their hearts to God, thereby experiencing the sanctifying influence that flows from Him. They do not seek their own personal, private agendas but pursue the will of the eternal Principal, pleading for the strength to accomplish His designs.

Jesus, as the supreme agent of God the Father, was engaged in His Father's business. Christians have a similar appointment. We should rejoice in Christ and

---

[450] Heb. 6:10 (NKJV).
[451] Acts 5:41 (ASV).

praise His holy name continually. Our cup is truly full, and our souls should be filled with eternal gratitude. Our desire to praise His holy name should be infinite and immeasurable.

Acting in the name of Christ is a sacred trust. It demands solemn and sober thinking. The words we speak and the things we do are not ours alone. They are the words and deeds of our Leader. If we speak, act, or pray without the Spirit, if we teach the philosophies of men instead of the doctrine of God, if we carry out our Christian duty flippantly or lightly—and do it all in the name of the Lord—then we may be taking the name of God in vain.

Chapter Twenty-four

His Name... in Vain

The name of God is sacred. The Lord's Prayer begins with the words, "Our Father in heaven, Hallowed be Your name." [452] From Mount Sinai God commanded: "You shall not take the name of the Lord your God in vain, for the Lord will not hold him guiltless who takes his name in vain." [453] In a world where conscientious, decent, devout Christians would never conceive of sins like murder, theft, or adultery, the name of God is often taken in vain without even a second thought.

---

[452] Matt. 6:9 (NKJV).
[453] Exo. 20:7 (ASV).

Too often we hear the sacred name of Deity dragged through the gutter—through flippant, profane, or unclean speech. Good Christians who conscientiously obey commandments that pertain to interpersonal relationships often miss the mark regarding the sanctity of God's holy name. Life allows us to either be true to who and what we are by righteously taking upon us the name of God or to risk jeopardizing our marvelous inheritance if we take and use God's name in vain.

Alternate translations of Exodus 20:7 read:

"You shall not misuse the name of the Lord your God." [454]

"Do not use my name for evil purposes." [455]

"You must not make wrong use of the name of the Lord your God." [456]

"Never use the name of the LORD your God carelessly." [457]

"You shall not make wrongful use of the name of the Lord your God." [458]

---

[454] New International Version.
[455] Good News Translation.
[456] Revised English Bible.
[457] God's Word® Translation.
[458] New Revised Standard Version.

The original wording of the commandment to "not take the name of the Lord your God in vain" is informative and illuminating. The Hebrew word *Nasah*, as used in Exodus 20:7, is translated in English Bibles as "take." In other verses it translates as—to lift or lift up, to raise, to bear or carry as a burden, or to take or carry away unjustly. In this context, "taking" the name of God is to lift or hold up His name, or to bear His name like a banner, or to carry His name away from its proper context.

"Vain" is translated from the Hebrew word *Shav*, which means—empty, worthless, meaningless, or waste and disorder. Vain implies "emptiness—a wandering in shadows without substance, a life without the possibility of satisfaction." [459]

The most common violation of taking the name of Deity in vain is in the context of cursing or profaning. Paul teaches us that we "are the temple of God and that the Spirit of God dwells" in us. He then informs us that "If anyone defiles the temple of God, God will destroy him. For the temple of God is holy, which temple you are." [460]

According to Lewis & Short, de Vaan, etc., the word profane, from the Latin phrase *pro fano*, literally

---

[459] Richards, Lawrence O., *Expository Dictionary of Bible Words*, Zondervan, 1985, p 608.
[460] 1 Cor. 3:16, 17 (NKJV).

means "out in front of the temple" or "outside the temple." What an apropos description of profaning the holy name of God: taking what is most holy, removing it from its hallowed setting, and dumping it, as it were, in a setting that is unholy and unclean! This sin was so severe that ancient Israel regarded it as a crime worthy of capital punishment. The threat of death associated with taking God's name in vain has long since disappeared, but the seriousness of the sin has not changed, and the Lord has stated that those taking His name in vain shall not be held guiltless.

We take the name of the Lord in vain when we use the sacred names of God the Father and His Son, Jesus Christ, profanely: in hateful cursing, in angry criticisms, accusations, and condemnations, or even as simple marks of punctuation in everyday speech. However, taking the name of God in vain entails much more than profaning His name, cursing, or blaspheming. Refraining from profanity or blasphemy is not enough. We need to emphasize the importance of the Lord's holy name in our personal lives. Our speech as well as our actions should leave no doubt that we are followers of Jesus Christ. Obedience to the third commandment has as much to do with the way we live and the way we are as it does with the way we speak.

As Christians we have been called to live our lives in a manner that would bring dignity and respect to the sacred name of God. If we love the Lord, we will cherish His word and always act and speak with deferential reverence toward Deity.

The growing amount of profanity and vulgarity in movies, music, television, books, and the Internet is a sad and sobering commentary on our times. Our inhumanity to others is certainly related to our neglect of sacred matters. Society's increasing callousness, crudeness, and inconsiderateness is certainly connected with denying, defying, and ignoring God.

Ancient Israel transgressed His laws, changed His ordinances, broke His everlasting covenants [461] and pursued false gods. They desecrated His sacred name and later felt the chastisement of God as they lost their land and were scattered among nations and people. Still, Ezekiel foretold a time of future hope:

"But I had concern for my holy name, which the house of Israel had profaned among the nations to which they came.

"...It is not for your sake, O house of Israel, that I am about to act, but for the sake of my holy name, which you have profaned among the nations to which you came.

---

[461] Isa. 24:5.

"And I will vindicate the holiness of my great name, which has been profaned among the nations, and which you have profaned among them. And the nations will know that I am the Lord, declares the Lord God, when through you I vindicate my holiness before their eyes." [462]

Then God promised to cleanse them and to give them a "new heart" and a "new spirit." [463] It is an honor to know Jesus and, through Him, the Father. We can rejoice in our divine birthright and in the privilege and possibility of taking on us the name of Christ.

When we speak Christ's name, we should do it with the deepest reverence.

---

[462] Eze. 36:21-23 (ESV).
[463] Ibid. 25.

Chapter Twenty-five

Biblical Names of God

The names and titles of God are descriptions of who God is, what He does and what He means to us, His beloved children. These names give us an amazing understanding of how incredibly wonderful God is in His varying roles. He is almighty, holy, powerful. His appearance can be terrible and frightening, yet He is tender, compassionate, faithful, full of grace and mercy.

Jesus Christ is the Lamb of God who gave His life as a sacrifice for mankind. He is also the roaring Lion of the tribe of Judah who devours His enemies.

Many of us only want to know Jesus as the Lamb or the Good Shepherd, the kind and forgiving healer.

But Jesus is also the fierce and consuming Lion who roars from Zion through the mouth of His prophets. Jesus Christ is both comforting and terrifying. He offers us His amazing grace, yet He demands purity and holiness. He is our best friend and our exalted King.

As we read through all the names and titles of God, we should ask the holy Spirit to open our eyes, our minds, and our hearts and to reveal to our spirit who God truly is, in all His majesty, love and wisdom.

A

ABBA (Romans 8:15)

ADVOCATE (I John 2:1 KJV)

ALMIGHTY (Genesis 17:1)

ALL IN ALL (Colossians 3:11)

ALPHA (Revelation 22:13)

AMEN (Revelation 3:14)

ANCIENT OF DAYS (Daniel 7:9)

ANOINTED ONE (Psalm 2:2)

APOSTLE (Hebrews 3:1)

ARM OF THE LORD (Isaiah 53:1)

AUTHOR OF ETERNAL SALVATION (Hebrews 5:9)

AUTHOR OF OUR FAITH (Hebrews 12:2)

AUTHOR OF PEACE (1 Cor. 14:33)

AVENGER (1 Thessalonians 4:6)

B

BEGINNING (Revelation 21:6)

BISHOP OF SOULS (1 Peter 2:25)

BLESSED & HOLY RULER (1 Timothy 6:15)

BRANCH (Jeremiah 33:15)

BREAD OF GOD (John 6:33)

BREAD OF LIFE (John 6:35)

BREATH OF LIFE (Genesis 2:7, Rev. 11:11)

BRIDEGROOM (Isaiah 62:5)

BRIGHT MORNING STAR (Revelation 22:16)

BUCKLER (2 Sam.22:31, Psalm 18:2, Psalm 18:30, Proverbs 2:7 KJVs)

C

CAPTAIN OF SALVATION (Hebrews 2:10)

CARPENTER (Mark 6:3)

CHIEF SHEPHERD (1 Peter 5:4)

CHOSEN ONE (Isaiah 42:1)

CHRIST (Matthew 22:42)

CHRIST OF GOD (Luke 9:20)

CHRIST THE LORD (Luke 2:11)

CHRIST, SON OF THE LIVING GOD (Matt. 16:16)

COMFORTER (John 14:26 KJV)

COMMANDER (Isaiah 55:4)

CONSOLATION OF ISRAEL (Luke 2:25)

CONSUMING FIRE (Deut. 4:24, Heb. 12:29)

CORNERSTONE (Isaiah 28:16)

COUNSELOR (Isaiah 9:6)

CREATOR (1 Peter 4:19)

CROWN OF BEAUTY (Isaiah 28:5)

D

DAYSPRING (Luke 1:78)

DELIVERER (Romans 11:26)

DESIRED OF ALL NATIONS (Haggai 2:7)

DIADEM OF BEAUTY (Isaiah 28:5)

DOOR (John 10:7 KJV)

DWELLING PLACE (Psalm 90:1)

E

ELECT ONE (Isaiah 42:1)

EMMANUEL (Matthew 1:23 KJV)

END (Revelation 21:6)

ETERNAL GOD (Deut. 33:27)

ETERNAL LIFE (1 John 5:20)

ETERNAL SPIRIT (Hebrews 9:14)

EVERLASTING FATHER (Isaiah 9:6)

EVERLASTING GOD (Genesis 21:33)

EXCELLENT (Psalm 148:13 KJV)

F

FAITHFUL AND TRUE (Revelation 19:11)

FAITHFUL WITNESS (Revelation 1:5)

FATHER (Matthew 6:9)

FIRSTBORN (Rom.8:29, Rev.1:5, Col.1:15)

FIRSTFRUITS (1 Cor.15:20-23)

FORTRESS (Jeremiah 16:19)

FOUNDATION (1 Cor. 3:11)

FOUNTAIN OF LIVING WATERS (Jeremiah 2:13)

FRIEND (Matthew 11:19)

FULLERS' SOAP (Malachi 3:2 KJV)

G

GENTLE WHISPER (1 Kings 19:12)

GIFT OF GOD (John 4:10)

GLORY OF THE LORD (Isaiah 40:5)

GOD (Genesis 1:1)

GOD ALMIGHTY (Genesis 17:1)

GOD OF THE WHOLE EARTH (Isaiah 54:5)

GOD OVER ALL (Romans 9:5)

GOD WHO SEES ME (Genesis 16:13)

GOODNESS (Psalm 144:2 KJV)

GOOD SHEPHERD (John 10:11)

GOVERNOR (Psalm 22:28 KJV)

GREAT HIGH PRIEST (Hebrews 4:14)

GREAT SHEPHERD (Hebrews 13:20)

GUIDE (Psalm 48:14)

H

HEAD OF THE BODY (Colossians 1:18)

HEAD OF THE CHURCH (Ephesians 5:23)

HEIR OF ALL THINGS (Hebrews 1:2)

HIDING PLACE (Psalm 32:7)

HIGHEST (Luke 1:76)

HIGH PRIEST (Hebrews 3:1)

HIGH PRIEST FOREVER (Hebrews 6:20)

HOLY GHOST (John 14:26)

HOLY ONE (Acts 2:27)

HOLY ONE OF ISRAEL (Isaiah 49:7)

HOLY SPIRIT (John 15:26)

HOPE (Titus 2:13)

HORN OF SALVATION (Luke 1:69)

HUSBAND (Isaiah 54:5, Jer. 31:32, Hosea 2:16)

I

I AM (Exodus 3:14, John 8:58)

IMAGE OF GOD (2 Cor. 4:4)

IMAGE OF HIS PERSON (Hebrews 1:3 KJV)

IMMANUEL (Isaiah 7:14)

INTERCESSOR (Rom. 8:26,27,34 Heb. 7:25)

J

JAH (Psalm 68:4 KJV)

JEALOUS (Exodus 34:14 KJV)

JEHOVAH (Psalm 83:18 KJV)

JESUS (Matthew 1:21)

JESUS CHRIST OUR LORD (Romans 6:23)

JUDGE (Isaiah 33:22, Acts 10:42)

JUST ONE (Acts 22:14)

K

KEEPER (Psalm 121:5)

KING (Zechariah 9:9)

KING ETERNAL (1 Timothy 1:17)

KING OF GLORY (Psalm 24:10)

KING OF THE JEWS (Matthew 27:11)

KING OF KINGS (1 Timothy 6:15)

KING OF SAINTS (Revelation 15:3)

L

LAMB OF GOD (John 1:29)

LAST ADAM (1 Cor. 15:45)

LAWGIVER (Isaiah 33:22)

LEADER (Isaiah 55:4)

LIFE (John 14:6)

LIGHT OF THE WORLD (John 8:12)

LIKE AN EAGLE (Deut. 32:11)

LILY OF THE VALLEYS (Song 2:1)

LION OF THE TRIBE OF JUDAH (Revelation 5:5)

LIVING GOD (Daniel 6:20)

LIVING STONE (1 Peter 2:4)

LIVING WATER (John 4:10)

LORD (John 13:13)

LORD GOD ALMIGHTY (Revelation 15:3)

LORD GOD OF HOSTS (Jeremiah 15:16)

LORD JESUS CHRIST (1 Cor. 15:57)

LORD OF ALL (Acts 10:36)

LORD OF GLORY (1 Cor. 2:8)

LORD OF HARVEST (Matthew 9:38)

LORD OF HOSTS (Haggai 1:5)

LORD OF LORDS (1 Tim. 6:15)

LORD OUR RIGHTEOUSNESS (Jeremiah 23:6)

LOVE (1 John 4:8)

LOVINGKINDNESS (Psalm 144:2)

M

MAKER (Job 35:10, Psalm 95:6)

MAJESTY ON HIGH (Hebrews 1:3)

MAN OF SORROWS (Isaiah 53:3)

MASTER (Luke 5:5)

MEDIATOR (1 Timothy 2:5)

MERCIFUL GOD (Jeremiah 3:12)

MESSENGER OF THE COVENANT (Malachi 3:1)

MESSIAH (John 4:25)

MIGHTY GOD (Isaiah 9:6)

MIGHTY ONE (Isaiah 60:16)

MOST UPRIGHT (Isaiah 26:7)

N

NAZARENE (Matthew 2:23)

O

OFFSPRING OF DAVID (Revelation 22:16)

OMEGA (Revelation 22:13)

ONLY BEGOTTEN SON (John 1:18 KJV)

OUR PASSOVER LAMB (1 Cor. 5:7)

OUR PEACE (Ephesians 2:14)

P

PHYSICIAN (Luke 4:23)

PORTION (Psalm 73:26, Psalm 119:57)

POTENTATE (1 Timothy 6:15)

POTTER (Isaiah 64:8)

POWER OF GOD (1 Cor. 1:24)

PRINCE OF LIFE (Acts 3:15)

PRINCE OF PEACE (Isaiah 9:6)

PROPHET (Acts 3:22)

PROPHET OF THE HIGHEST (Luke 1:76)

PROPITIATION (1 John 2:2, 1John 4:10)

PURIFIER (Malachi 3:3)

Q

QUICKENING SPIRIT (1 Corinthians 15:45 KJV)

R

RABBONI (TEACHER) (John 20:16)

RADIANCE OF GOD'S GLORY (Heb.1:3)

REDEEMER (Job 19:25)

REFINER'S FIRE (Malachi 3:2)

REFUGE (Jeremiah 16:19)

RESURRECTION (John 11:25)

REWARDER (Hebrews 11:6)

RIGHTEOUS ONE (1 John 2:1)

ROCK (1 Cor.10:4)

ROOT OF DAVID (Rev. 22:16)

ROSE OF SHARON (Song 2:1)

RULER OF GOD'S CREATION (Rev. 3:14)

RULER OVER KINGS OF EARTH (Rev 1:5)

RULER OVER ISRAEL (Micah 5:2)

S

SAVIOR (Luke 2:11)

SCEPTRE (Numbers 24:17)

SEED (Genesis 3:15)

SERVANT (Isaiah 42:1)

SHADE (Psalm 121:5)

SHEPHERD OF OUR SOULS (1Peter 2:25)

SHIELD (Genesis 15:1)

SHILOH (Genesis 49:10)

SONG (Exodus 15:2, Isaiah 12:2)

SON OF DAVID (Matthew 1:1)

SON OF GOD (Matthew 27:54)

SON OF MAN (Matthew 8:20)

SON OF THE MOST HIGH (Luke 1:32)

SOURCE (Hebrews 5:9)

SPIRIT (John 4:24)

SPIRIT OF ADOPTION (Romans 8:15)

SPIRIT OF GOD (Genesis 1:2)

SPIRIT OF TRUTH (John 14:17,15:26,16:13)

STAR OUT OF JACOB (Numbers 24:17)

STRENGTH (Jeremiah 16:19)

STONE (1 Peter 2:8)

STONE OF ISRAEL (Genesis 49:24)

STRONGHOLD (Nahum 1:7)

STRONG TOWER (Proverbs 18:10)

SUN OF RIGHTEOUSNESS (Malachi 4:2)

T

TEACHER (John 13:13)

TEMPLE (Revelation 21:22)

THE ONE (Psalm 144:2,10)

TRUE LIGHT (John 1:9)

TRUE WITNESS (Revelation 3:14)

TRUTH (John 14:6)

V

VINE (John 15:5)

W

WALL OF FIRE (Zechariah 2:5)

WAY (John 14:6)

WISDOM OF GOD (1 Cor. 1:24)

WITNESS (Isaiah 55:4)

WONDERFUL (Isaiah 9:6)

WORD (John 1:1)

WORD OF GOD (Revelation 19:13)

Y

YAH (Isaiah 12:2 KJV, Psalm 68:4 NKJV)

A Final Word

I sincerely hope you have enjoyed this journey of exploration through a portion of the many sacred names of God. I have certainly developed a greater insight into the God we worship as a result of writing this book.

I would be so grateful if you could post a review on Amazon or any other book site where you have posting privileges. Perhaps you could mention which one of God's holy names resonates most with you.

If you email me a link to your review, I would be happy to send you a free e-book of any one of my Powerful Christian Book Series. Just indicate to me which book you would most like to read: *Turning Faith into Power, Gaining Power through Prayer, The Added Power of Obedience, The Healing Power of Forgiveness,* or *The Mighty Power of the Word.*

Also, drop me a line if you spot any typos which may have escaped the eagle-eye of my proof-reader or if you have questions or want to offer any private feedback.

You can also follow me on twitter at: https://twitter.com/richthruchrist. I will definitely attempt to follow back. If you found this book inspiring, insightful, or simply enjoyable, I would love it if you could spread the word so that others may benefit from reading it as well.

Best wishes and may God bless you always!

Rich Nelson

P.S. I am including a free sample chapter from: *Sustainable Spirituality: Maintaining Faith in the Face of Adversity* at the end of this book.

About the Author

Rich Nelson is the author of numerous publications, including books, blogs, and articles on topics such as religious education, family values, health, and politics. His work has appeared in *Christian Education Today, Church Teacher, Parish Teacher, Living with Teenagers, Liberty Magazine,* and many others.

Contact Information:

Broken Hill Publications
Glenwood Springs, CO 91601

Email Rich at: rich@greenstemmedia.com

Visit Rich at: www.srnelson.com

Other Books by S. Richard Nelson

The Powerful Christian Series:

    Turning Faith into Power

    Gaining Power through Prayer

    The Added Power of Obedience

    The Healing Power of Forgiveness

    The Mighty Power of the Word

    The Gift and Power of the Holy Spirit

    Love: The Only True Power

Sustainable Spirituality

The Faith Factor

Sample Chapter:

II. SUSTAINABLE THROUGH THE STORMS

Eighty miles north of Jerusalem sits a resplendent lake known in biblical times as the Sea of Kinnereth or the Lake of Gennesaret. It is a freshwater lake about twelve miles long and seven miles wide that is fed by the Jordan River. Today, we refer to it as the Sea of Galilee.

The Sea of Galilee is the lake Jesus knew as a child. Its fertile western shore is situated about fifteen miles from his hometown of Nazareth. The Sea of Galilee and the adjacent Galilean hills provided a refuse where Jesus could so often return during the arduous days of his ministry.

Jesus frequently taught crowds of faithful followers and interested by-standers along the shores of Galilee. As the crowds pushed against him, Jesus would climb into a boat and push out a few yards to sea. Remaining close to shore, the master Teacher could then be more easily seen and heard by those straining to catch his powerful instruction.

The Sea of Galilee is situated about 680 feet below sea level with hills that rise sharply against the sky. The peaceful calm of the sea can change quite unexpectedly. Winds that funnel through the Galilean hill country can suddenly stir up the waters, but the more severe winds off the Golan Heights can be deadly. Cold air rushing down from the hills meets the warmer air rising off the lake and creates sudden, fleeting storms with ten-foot-high waves on the surface of the sea.

On one such evening, Jesus, after imparting his message to the crowds, set out with his disciples toward the opposite shore of the lake. Mark described what happened when "a great windstorm developed and the waves were breaking into the boat, so that the boat was nearly swamped.

"But he was in the stern, sleeping on a cushion. They woke him up and said to him, 'Teacher, don't you care that we are about to die?'

"So he got up and rebuked the wind, and said to the sea, 'Be quiet! Calm down!' Then the wind stopped and it was dead calm.

"And he said to them, 'Why are you cowardly? Do you still not have faith?'

"They were overwhelmed with fear and said to one another, 'Who then is this? Even the wind and sea obey him!'" [464]

In Genesis, God commanded; "Let there be an expanse in the midst of the waters and let it separate water from water." [465] He also ordered "the water

---

[464] Mark 4:37-41 (NET).
[465] Genesis 1:6 (NET).

under the sky be gathered into one place and let dry ground appear. And it was so." [466] In Exodus, he parted the Red Sea, allowing the Israelites to cross over on dry ground. [467] It certainly shouldn't surprise us that he could calm a simple storm on the Sea of Galilee.

We have all had sudden storms in our lives which seemingly appear out of nowhere. At times these temporary, fleeting storms can seem as devastating and frightening and potentially destructive as the storms of Galilee. In our personal lives, in our families, in our communities and even in our country, we have seen squalls arise that make us wonder, "Teacher, don't you care that we are about to die?" But always, in the stillness after the storm we sense somehow the words of the Master, "Why are you cowardly? Do you still not have faith?"

---

[466] Genesis 1:9 (NET).
[467] See Exodus 14:21, 22.

No one likes being called a coward and none of us would like to think that we don't have faith, but Jesus' soft scolding may be slightly deserved. Our faith should be our reminder that Christ can calm the troubled seas of our lives as easily as he calmed the Sea of Galilee.

I am reasonably certain that we will all experience hardship and misfortune over the course of our lifetimes. It seems none of us is immune. Some difficulties may be brutal, cruel, and potentially destructive. It could even make us question our faith in God.

But Jesus has pre-warned us that in this world we would "have trouble and suffering, but take courage – I have conquered the world." [468] He also promised: "Peace I leave with you; my peace I give to you. I do not give it to you as the world does. Do not

---

[468] John 16:33 (NET).

let your hearts be distressed or lacking in courage." [469]

On another evening, Jesus' disciples set out on a voyage across the same Sea of Galilee. Again, the wind became fierce and frightful, the waves bold and boisterous. The desperate disciples were worried because, this time, no one sailed with them who could calm the storm. Jesus had been left alone on the shore.

The boat was far from land and the violent waves and wind were beating against it. Suddenly, as the night was ending, the disciples perceived in the darkness a fluttering robe walking toward them on the waves of the sea. Believing it was a phantom that moved on the water, terror struck at their hearts. But Jesus called to them through the tempest and the darkness—just as he so often calls to us when we feel closed off in obscurity and surrounded by the raging

---

[469] John 14:27 (NET).

storms of life—with a reassuring and peaceful declaration, "Have courage! It is I. Do not be afraid."

Peter shouted, "Lord, if it is you, order me to come to you on the water." Jesus' simple answer to him was what he says to all of us: "Come."

And so, Peter climbed out of the boat and onto the turbulent sea. He must have been aware of the storm around him and felt the harsh waves splashing at his feet but while he kept his eyes fixed on the Savior, he was fine. When he removed his eyes from Christ and saw the dark and frightening waves beneath him, fear took hold and he started to sink.

Like us, when we are sinking into despair and drowning in our troubles, Peter called out: "Lord, save me!" Jesus immediately reached out his hand and caught the drowning disciple. "You of little faith," Jesus gently rebuked, "why did you doubt?" Safely back on board, the wind stopped, the rage became a ripple and the boat sailed on to the land of Gennesaret. [470]

Jesus is the one truly infallible light on the stormy sea of life. A light to the world, Jesus is the one unfailing beacon. He is "the way, the truth, and the life." [471] With our eyes fixed securely on him, we can walk safely over the waves of worry and despair. When we focus on the force and fierceness of the destructive influences around us, as we are so easily tempted to do in this world, we inevitably sink in a sea of conflict, sorrow, and hopelessness.

On the shore of peace and tranquility, Jesus Christ is the only dependable beacon on which we can firmly rely. When we feel the floods threatening to drown us and the waves eager to devour the tiny, tossed vessel of our faith, during the darkest hours of our storm the comforting words of Christ resonate

---

[470] See Matthew 14:22-33.
[471] John 14:6 (KJV).

within our hearts: "Have courage! It is I. Do not be afraid." [472]

Sustaining Hope

After Moses gave the laws and the commandments to the ancient Israelites, the Lord told them: "Today I invoke heaven and earth as a witness against you that I have set life and death, blessing and curse, before you. Therefore, choose life so that you and your descendants may live!

"I also call on you to love the Lord your God, to obey him and be loyal to him, for he gives you life and enables you to live continually in the land the Lord promised to give to your ancestors Abraham, Isaac, and Jacob." [473]

The source of sustainable hope is the source of life.

---

[472] Matthew 14:27 (NET).
[473] Deuteronomy 30:19, 20 (NET).

Hope is one of the three great Christian virtues.

Hope will endure in the human heart even when all odds are against it. When our own knowledge, judgment and experience tell us there is no reason to hope, hope will persist.

To choose hope is to choose life. The choice offered by the Lord your God is life, and life offers hope. Hope in Christ offers hope in the future. Our ordinary, everyday hope can become so strong, so versatile and so sustainable that worthlessness and despair could not exist within us. When we choose Christ, we literally cannot despair unless we consciously decide to do so.

Death may be entangled with life, but we still choose to either feed darkness and death, or we choose to feed brightness and hope. We can choose to worry away our lives. We can refuse the light of Jesus Christ. Piece by piece, a little at a time, we can give our lives over to the devil until we no longer have the power to wrench them free again. We can strangle all our hopes until meaninglessness and despair overcome us. But it must be a conscientious choice.

Christ submitted himself to death but, "has been raised from the dead, he is never going to die again; death no longer has mastery over him". [474] Jesus is the master of life and the master over death. Any choice other than Christ is a choice of spiritual death. Physical death has no power over him, and in the end will have no power over us through Christ.

Life and hope are always stronger than death. If we choose hope, we set in motion powerful spiritual forces for life. Jesus Christ responds to those tender tendrils of crippled life with the force and energy that will bring them to flowering.

---

[474] Romans 6:9 (NET).

We can choose hope in the depths of despair. We can choose growth in the midst of oppression. We can choose understanding in the presence of ignorance. We can choose love in the arms of violence and hatred. We can choose to forgive, to pray, to be kind, to help each other. When we do, we will feel Christ's abundant love. He sees every kindness to even the poorest human creature as a kindness to him. In exchange, he adds hope, strength, joy and meaning to our lives.

Paul asked, "Who will separate us from the love of Christ? Will trouble, or distress, or persecution, or famine, or nakedness, or danger, or sword?

".... No, in all these things we have complete victory through him who loved us.

"For I am convinced that neither death, nor life, nor angels, nor heavenly rulers, nor things that are present, nor things to come, nor powers, "nor height, nor depth, nor anything else in creation will be able to separate us from the love of God in Christ Jesus our Lord." [475]

Christ is our only sustainable hope. He is our hope during our darkest nights. He is our hope on those miserable Monday mornings. He is our hope when depression and despair darken our doorway. Jesus has declared: "I am the door. If anyone enters through me, he will be saved." [476] Despair is the thief of life. Depression comes only to steal, and to kill, and to destroy. But Jesus has come that we may have life and may have it abundantly. He is the good shepherd, and he assures us: "The good shepherd lays down his life for the sheep." [477]

---

[475] Romans 8:35-39 (NET).
[476] John 10:9 (NET).
[477] See John 10:9-11.

From the book:

Sustainable Spirituality:
Maintaining Faith in the Face of Adversity

Available on Amazon.

www.ingramcontent.com/pod-product-compliance
Lightning Source LLC
Chambersburg PA
CBHW060149050426
42446CB00013B/2733